Mark Ravenhill's first full-length play, *Shopping and Fucking*, produced by Out of Joint and the Royal Court Theatre, opened at the Royal Court Theatre Upstairs in September 1996 and was followed by a national tour. It transferred to the Queen's Theatre in the West End in June 1997 and was followed by an international tour. His second play, *Faust is Dead*, was produced by Actors' Touring Company (national tour) in 1997. *Sleeping Around*, a joint venture with three other writers, opened at the Salisbury Playhouse in February 1998 before a run at the Donmar Warehouse, London, followed by a national tour. *Handbag* was produced by Actors' Touring Company in 1998. *Some Explicit Polaroids*, for Out of Joint, opened at the Theatre Royal, Bury St Edmunds, followed by a run at the New Ambassadors, London, in October 1999. All the plays have been widely translated and produced across the world.

Methuen

5 7 9 10 8 6 4

First published in Great Britain in 2001 by
Methuen Publishing Limited

This edition published in 2002 by
Methuen Publishing Limited,
11–12 Buckingham Gate,
London SW1E 6LB

Copyright © 2001 Mark Ravenhill
Song lyrics copyright © 2001 Mark Ravenhill
Music © 2001 Matthew Scott

The author has asserted his moral rights.

Methuen Publishing Limited Reg. No. 3543167

A CIP catalogue record for this book is available from the British Library

ISBN 10: 0 413 76930 5
ISBN 13: 978-0-413-76930-5

Typeset by SX Composing DTP, Rayleigh, Essex
Printed and bound in Great Britain by
Cox & Wyman Ltd, Reading, Berkshire

Caution

Mother Clap's Molly House

A play with songs by
Mark Ravenhill

Music by **Matthew Scott**

Methuen Drama

background by arrangement with Michael Codron for Nederlander Theatres (Aldwych) Ltd, presents

NT The Royal National Theatre production of

Mother Clap's Molly House

A play with songs by **Mark Ravenhill**
Music by **Matthew Scott**
Directed by **Nicholas Hytner**

MOTHER CLAP'S MOLLY HOUSE

a play with songs by **Mark Ravenhill**
music by **Matthew Scott**

MRS TULL	**DEBORAH FINDLAY**
STEPHEN TULL	**IAIN MITCHELL**
MARTIN, *THEIR APPRENTICE*	**PAUL READY**
PRINCESS SERAPHINA	**ROBERT BLYTHE**

WHORES

AMELIA	**MAGGIE McCARTHY**
AMY	**DANIELLE TILLEY**
MARY CRANTON	**DEBBIE CHAZEN**
MARY BOLTON	**KATY SECOMBE**

WORKING MEN

KEDGER	**JAY SIMPSON**
PHILIPS	**WILLIAM OSBORNE**
THOMAS, *THEIR APPRENTICE*	**TOM McKAY**
GABRIEL LAWRENCE	**CON O'NEILL**

DEITIES

GOD	**DANIEL REDMOND**
EROS	**NEIL COUPERTHWAITE**

JOSH	**TOM McKAY**
WILL	**WILLIAM OSBORNE**
CHARLIE	**JAY SIMPSON**
TINA	**DANIELLE TILLEY**
TOM	**PAUL READY**
EDWARD	**IAIN MITCHELL**
PHIL	**CON O'NEILL**

OTHER PARTS PLAYED BY
**DEBORAH ASANTE, ANTHONY MARK BARROW,
JACK BENNETT, PAMELA HARDMAN, AIDAN MEECH, IAIN PEARSON,
PHILIP RALPH, ALI SICHILONGO**

MUSICIANS

KEYBOARD/MUSIC DIRECTOR	**MATTHEW SCOTT**
ASSOCIATE MUSIC DIRECTOR	**MICHAEL HASLAM**
SAXOPHONE	**THOMAS BOWLES**
GUITARS	**BEN GROVE**
SAXOPHONE	**SIMON HARAM**
PERCUSSION	**PHILIP HOPKINS**

DIRECTOR	**NICHOLAS HYTNER**
SET DESIGNER	**GILES CADLE**
COSTUME DESIGNER	**NICKY GILLIBRAND**
LIGHTING DESIGNER	**RICK FISHER**
MUSIC DIRECTOR	**MATTHEW SCOTT**
DIRECTOR OF MOVEMENT	**JANE GIBSON**
SOUND DESIGNERS	**NEIL ALEXANDER, COLIN PINK**
CASTING DIRECTOR	**GABRIELLE DAWES**
COMPANY VOICE WORK	**PATSY RODENBURG**
PRODUCTION PHOTOGRAPHER	**MARK DOUET**

Staff Director	**Crispin Bonham Carter**
General Manager	**Sid Higgins**
Production Manager for **background**	**Paul Hennessy**
Company Stage Manager	**Helen Barratt**
Deputy Stage Manager	**Stuart Calder**
Assistant Stage Manager	**Amy Howden**
Assistant to the Lighting Designer	**Paul McLeish**
Costume Supervisor	**Donna Guadagnini**
Wardrobe Manager	**Kathryn Waters**

**First performance at the National's Lyttelton Theatre: 4 September 2001
First performance at Aldwych Theatre: 8 February 2002**

**Length: about 2 hours 30 minutes,
including 20-minute interval**

The play was first commissioned and presented in
a workshop production by the London Academy of Music
and Dramatic Arts in February 2000

Detail from
Hogarth's *Credulity,
Superstition and
Fanaticism*, 1762

DEBORAH ASANTE
(ENSEMBLE)

Deborah Asante trained at the London Centre for Theatre Studies and the City Lit. Recent **theatre** includes *The Good Woman of Setzuan* for NT Education, *The Lottie Project* for Polka Children's Theatre, *Bonded*, a national tour for Tiata Fahodzi, a British West African theatre company, *Three Lords and Ladies of London* for the Globe's education department/National Black Theatre Co, Ophelia in *Hamlet* at the Orange Tree, and Mrs Jackson in *The Amen Corner* at Bristol Old Vic. **Film** and **TV** includes *A Mother's Revenge*, *The Bill*, *Bad Boyz Blue* and *Life of Riley*. **Radio**: *The Fortune Teller of Babubu* and *Text Message*.

ANTHONY MARK BARROW
(ENSEMBLE)

Anthony Mark Barrow trained at Central School of Speach and Drama. His **theatre** credits include: *Lady Salsa*, Talk of the Town, London, *Macbeth* and *The Tempest*, Edinburgh Festival 1999, *Lettuce and Lovage*, Alexandra, Birmingham. **TV** credits include: *Murder in Mind*, *Oscar Charlie*, *Holby City*, *Down to Earth* and *Well Schooled in Murder*. **Film** includes: *Plato's Breaking Point*, *10/34*.

JACK BENNETT
(ENSEMBLE)

Jack Bennett trained at LAMDA, graduating in 2001. His **theatre** credits include Mike in *Lie of the Mind* and James in *The Strangeness of Others* at LAMDA. This is Jack's first professional theatre engagement.

ROBERT BLYTHE
(PRINCESS SERAPHINA)

Theatre work includes: repertory seasons at Swansea Grand, Theatr Clwyd, Leicester Haymarket, Cardiff Sherman, Liverpool Playhouse and Worthing Connaught. He has also toured the Far East, Middle East, India and Europe. Most recent theatre: *The Norman Conquests*, *King Lear*, *Bedroom Farce* and *The Rabbit* all for Terry Hands at Clwyd Theatre Cymru, Mold. Teddy in *House & Garden* for Alan Ayckbourn at The Stephen Joseph Theatre, Scarborough and *Ghosts* for Greg Herzof at The Royal Exchange Theatre, Manchester. Most recent London theatre: *Badfinger* at the Donmar Warehouse, *Under Milk Wood* at the Royal National Theatre and *Heaven* at The Lilian Baylis. Recent **television** work includes: *The Governor*, *Dangerous Lady*, *The Biz*, *The Lifeboat*, *The Preston Front*, *Delta Wave Expert Witness*, *Casualty*, *The Bill*, *Middlemarch*, *EastEnders*, *Oliver's Travels*, *Harri Webb*, *Outside Time*, *Coronations Street*, *The Famous Five*, *The Broker's Man*, *Heatbeat*, *Mortimer's Law*, the pilot episode for a new BBC sitcom *High Hopes*, *The Secret Life of Michael Fry*, *Belonging*, *Waking the Dead* and *Without Motive*. **Film** work includes: *The Theory of Flight*, *The Woodlanders*, *Darklands*, *The Englishman Who Went Up a Hill But Came Down a Mountain*, *The Love Child*, *Rebecca's Daughters*, *Whoops Apocalypse*, *And Nothing but the Truth* and *Experience Preferred But Not Essential*.

DEBBIE CHAZEN
(MARY CRANTON)

Debbie Chazen trained at LAMDA. Her **theatre** credits include *The Knife* at the NT's Studio, *Frogs* at Nottingham Playhouse, *The Rise and Fall of Little Voice* at Salisbury Playhouse and *A Midsummer Night's Dream* in the West End. **TV**: *Nicholas Nickleby*, *Gimme, Gimme, Gimme*, *The Lakes*, *An Unsuitable Job for a Woman*, *Killernet*, *Tess of the D'Urbervilles*, *Ruth Rendell: You Can't Be Too Careful*, *Midsomer Murders*, *The Bill*, *A Christmas Carol*, *Lucy Sullivan is Getting Married* and *Casualty*. **Film**: *The Rendezvous*, *Topsy-Turvy*, *Beginner's Luck* and *Barnie et ses petites contrariétés*. **Radio**: *Dinner Ladies*.

NEIL COUPERTHWAITE
(EROS)

Neil trained at the Arts Educational School where he was awarded the Andrew Lloyd Webber Scholarship. After drama school he went straight into the original West End production of *Moby Dick* at the Piccadilly Theatre. Neil recently performed as Angel in the new production of *Rent* at the Prince of Wales Theatre, London, other work in the West End includes *Hot Mikado* at the Queen's Theatre, Doody in *Grease* at both the Dominion, Cambridge Theatres, London and Sweden, and the lead role of Rusty in *Starlight Express* at the Apollo Victoria Theatre, London and in Bochum, Germany. Other theatre credits include *Cabaret* at the Arts Theatre, Belfast, *Scrooge* at the Alexandra Theatre, Birmingham, *A Slice of Saturday Night* at the Mercury Theatre, Colchester, *Les Misérables* at the Point Theatre, Dublin and the Playhouse Theatre, Edinburgh and Rusty in *Starlight Express* in Bochum, Germany. **TV** includes Daniel in *Deidre's Dilemma* for the BBC.

DEBORAH FINDLAY
(MRS TULL)

Deborah Findlay's **theatre** credits include *Once in a While* and *The Winter's Tale* at the National, *Stanley* at the National and at Circle in the Square, New York (Olivier Award, Best Supporting Actress), *Commitments* and *Keyboard Skills* at the Bush, *The Threesome* at the Lyric, Hammersmith, *Artists and Admirers* at the Riverside Studios, *A Doll's House* and *The Crucible* at the Crucible, Sheffield, *Tom and Viv* and *Overgrown Paths* at the Royal Court, *Top Girls* at the Royal Court and at the Public Theatre, New York (OBIE award for her performance as Joyce and Isabella in New York), *Mrs Gauguin*, *Hedda Gabler* and *Tongue of a Bird* at the Almeida, *Macbeth* at the Nuffield, Southampton, *The House of Bernarda Alba* in the West End, *Three Sisters*, *The New Inn*, *Twelfth Night*, *The Merchant of Venice* and *The School for Scandal* for the RSC, *King Lear* and *As You Like It* for the Oxford Stage Company, *The Beaux' Stratagem* on tour and at Richmond, *The Clandestine Marriage* for Thelma Holt on tour and in the West End and *The Seagull* for Thelma Holt. **TV** includes *What if it's Raining?*, *First and Last*, *All Good Things*, *Top Girls*, *The House of Bernarda Alba*, *Downtown Lagos*, *Anglo Saxon Attitudes*, *Natural Lies*, *Maigret*, *Sherlock Holmes*, *Milner*, *Jane Eyre*, *Kavanagh QC*, *Trial and Retribution II*, *Wives and Daughters*, *The Midsomer Murders*, *Anna Karenina*, *Messiah*, and *Armstrong and Miller*. **Film**: *Truly Madly Deeply*, *Jack and Sarah*, *The End of the Affair* and *Me Without You*.

PAMELA HARDMAN (ENSEMBLE)

Pamela Hardman trained at Arts Educational School. Her **theatre** credits include *Suddenly At Home*, *September Tide* and *Murder Mistaken* at the Grand, Wolverhampton, *Murder Weekend* at the Theatre Royal, Brighton, *My Cousin Rachel*, *Who Killed Santa Claus?*, *I Have Been Here Before* and *Murder by the Book* for Pomegranate Theatre, *How the Other Half Loves* in Stockholm, *The Unvarnished Truth* at Sheringham Rep, *Miss Julie*, *Sherlock's Last Case*, *The Lover* and *Macbeth* at the Oldham Rep, *It Runs in the Family* and *Funny Money* at the Playhouse, *Black Comedy* and *The Real Inspector Hound* at the Comedy Theatre, and *Talking Heads* and *Lettice and Lovage* on UK tour.

MAGGIE McCARTHY
(AMELIA)

Maggie McCarthy's **theatre** credits in London include *Fanshen*, *The Shaughraun*, *The Night of the Iguana*, *Macbeth* and *Mountain Giants* at the National, *The Garden Girls* at the Bush for which she won a *Time Out* Performance Award, *The Crucible* at the Young Vic, *Golden Pathway Annual* at the Mayfair, *Amid the Standing Corn* at Soho Poly, *Byrthrite*, *The Seagull* and *Thickness of Skin* at the Royal Court, *The Steward of Christendom* for Out of Joint Theatre at the Royal Court, BAM New York, and The Gate, Dublin, *Cat with Green Violin* at the Orange Tree, *Sailor Beware* at the Lyric, Hammersmith, *The Storm* at the Almeida and *Drummers* for Out of Joint; and elsewhere, *The Merchant of Venice*, *Rose*, *The Atheist's Tragedy*, *Richard III*, *The Importance of Being Earnest*, *Mother Courage*, *Candida*, *Macbeth* and *Billy Liar* at the Belgrade, Coventry, *Clouds* at the Nuffield, Southampton, *All's Well that Ends Well* at the Birmingham Rep, *Space Invaders* and *Quartz* at the Traverse, Edinburgh, *Travesties*, *Stirrings in Sheffield*, *Twelfth Night*, *Getting On* and *Slag* at the Sheffield Crucible, *Scrape off the Black* at the West Yorkshire Playhouse, and *Misery* at the Leicester Haymarket. **TV**: *The Boot Street Band*, *She's Out*, *All Quiet on the Preston Front*, *Hello Girls*, *Berkeley Square* and *Trial and Retribution V*. **Film**: *Firelight*, *Hilary and Jackie*, *Angela's Ashes*, *Esther Khan* and *Ali-G in da House*. **Radio**: *The Archers*, *Citizens*, and many plays for Radio 3 and 4.

TOM McKAY
(THOMAS/JOSH)

Tom McKay graduated from LAMDA in July 2001. His first professional engagement was China Mary in *Mother Clap's Molly House* at the RNT's Lyttleton Theatre. Prior to LAMDA his theatre experience included for the RSC, *Edmund Ironside* (Fringe Festival), *Lord of the Flies* and *Macbeth*.

AIDAN MEECH
(ENSEMBLE)

Aidan Meech trained at the Royal Scottish Academy of Music and Drama. His **theatre** credits include *Romeo and Juliet* and *All That Trouble That We Had* at the New Vic Theatre, *Mrs Steinberg* and *The Byker Boy* at The Bush. Workshops of *Henry IV* at The Young Vic Theatre and *Fancies, Chaste and Noble* at the RNT Studio. *The Maids* for Theatre Informer,

Mary Queen of Scots Got Her Head Chopped Off for Northern Exposure, *Summoned* for Tron Theatre, Glasgow, *Antony and Cleopatra* for RSC, Newcastle tour, *The Importance of Being Earnest, Measure for Measure, The Oresteia, Saved* and *The Cherry Orchard* for Royal Scottish Academy of Music and Drama.
TV includes: 4 episodes of *Byker Grove* (BBC)

IAIN MITCHELL
(STEPHEN TULL/EDWARD)
Iain Mitchell studied at Guildhall School of Music. His work in **theatre** includes, for the National, *The Madness of George III, The Prince's Play, Marat/Sade, Chips with Everything, Flight, Battle Royal* and *Albert Speer,* and at the NT Studio: *The Rivals, Early Morning* and *Pericles.* Elsewhere, *Easy Virtue* at the Garrick, *The Scarlet Pimpernel* at Chichester and in the West End, *Hamlet* at the Warehouse and the Piccadilly, *Marya* at the Old Vic, *The Invention of Love* at the Theatre Royal, Haymarket (NT transfer), *Victory* for the Wrestling School, *School for Scandal, The Changeling, Macbeth* and *Home* for Cambridge Theatre Company, *Twelfth Night* and *Respectable Wedding* at Chichester, *Oliver Twist* at the Gate Theatre, Dublin and *The Tower* at the Almeida. For the RSC: *Henry V, Henry VI Parts 1,2 & 3, Othello, Coriolanus, Hamlet, The Comedy of Errors, Savage Amusement* and *Hang of the Gaol.*
TV includes *Cat's Eyes, A Sleeping Life, Allo Allo, Secret Weapon, You Rang M'Lord, Peak Practice, Lovejoy, Scarlet and Black, Milner, Bramwell, Alas Smith and Jones, Is It Legal?, Cracker, A Royal Scandal, Cows, Hippies* and *Murder in Mesopotamia.* **Film**: *Fierce Creatures, The Madness of King George, The Tenth Kingdom* and *The Parole Officer.*

CON O'NEILL
(GABRIEL LAWRENCE/PHIL)
Con O'Neill's **theatre** credits include *Riddley Walker* at the Royal Exchange, Manchester, *Blood Brothers* in the West End and on Broadway, for which he gained a Tony nomination and an Olivier for Most Outstanding Performance in a Musical, *The Awakening, The Fastest Clock, The Flight to Egypt* and *Featuring Loretta* at Hampstead, *Woyzeck* for Hull Truck Theatre, and *A Tribute to the Blues Brothers* at the Whitehall Theatre (which he co-wrote and co-produced), which gained an Olivier nomination for Best Entertainment. **TV**: *Norbert Smith, One Summer, Amongst Barbarians, The Riff Raff Element, Pie in the Sky, Casualty,*

Inspector Morse, Moving Story, Soldier Soldier, Peak Practice, Wycliffe, Tom Jones, Macbeth, Heartbeat, Cider with Rosie, Always and Everyone, Real Women II and *Waking the Dead.*
Film: *Dancin' Thru the Dark, The Lilac Bus, Scarborough Ahoy!, Three Steps to Heaven, A Perfect Match, Bedrooms and Hallways* and *The Last Seduction 2.* He wrote and directed the award-winning short film *Brotherly Love,* and his debut feature film script *Anam Cara* is in development with Revolution Films.

WILLIAM OSBORNE
(PHILIPS/WILL)
William Osborne trained at Central.
His **theatre** credits include *Absolute Hell, La Grande Magia, King Lear* and *Battle Royal* at the National, *Our Day Out* and *A Christmas Carol* at Nottingham Playhouse, *Joseph and his Amazing Technicolor Dreamcoat* at Leicester Haymarket, *As You Like It* at the Royal Exchange, Manchester, *Pravda, Hobson's Choice* and *All's Well That Ends Well* at Leeds Playhouse, *Rough Crossing* on tour, *Paris Match* at Theatr Clwyd, *Screamers* at the Arts Theatre, *The Secret Agent* for Etcetera Theatre, *The Last Enemy* for Gay Sweatshop, *The Case of the Frightened Lady* at the Palace Theatre, Watford, *The Deep Blue Sea* at the Almeida and Apollo, *The Rivals* at Chichester, the Albery and on tour, *The Strip* at the Royal Court and *The Misanthrope* at the Young Vic. **TV** includes *Have his Carcase, Rumpole of the Bailey, Victoria Wood Playhouse – Over to Pam, Poirot, Absolute Hell, Don't Leave Us This Way, Victoria Wood Christmas Special, Pie in the Sky, Fall from Grace, Cold Comfort Farm, The Bill, Brazen Hussies, As Time Goes By, Hot Stuff, Get Well Soon, King Lear, Wonderful You, Couples, The Tenth Kingdom* and *One Foot in the Grave.* **Film**: *Damage, Tom and Viv, Virtual Sexuality* and *Bedazzled.*

IAIN PEARSON
(ENSEMBLE)
Iain Pearson trained at RSAMD. His **theatre** credits include *The Playboy of the Western World* at the National, *Phaedra's Love* for Ghostown Theatre, *The Maids* for Dirty Dog Theatre, *Road* for Open Windows Theatre and *A.D* for Raindog. **TV**: *Rik Mayall Presents, Children's Ward, Coronation Street* and *Trial and Retribution.*

PHILIP RALPH
(ENSEMBLE)
Philip Ralph trained at RADA. His **theatre** work includes *Look Back in Anger* (understudy) at the National, *The Tempest* at the Mercury, Colchester, *The Threepenny Opera* at Bury St Edmunds and on tour, *Moments of Madness* for Volcano Theatre Co., *Othello* at the Theatre Royal, Bury St Edmunds, *Twelfth Night* for Imaginary Forces Tour, *Waiting for Godot* and *They're Playing our Song* for Brewhouse Theatre Company, *The Butcher of Baghdad* for Cherub Theatre Company, *Romeo and Juliet* at the Angles Centre Wisbech, *The Comedy of Errors* and *The Jolly Potters* at the New Victoria Theatre, Stoke. **TV** includes *Lawyers, The Vice, Dalziel and Pascoe, Castles, Degrees of Error* and *Pie in the Sky.*

PAUL READY
(MARTIN/TOM)
Paul Ready trained at LAMDA. His **theatre** credits include *Cuckoos* at the Gate (NT Springboards Season), *Twelfth Night* at the Liverpool Playhouse and Everyman and *The Beggar's Opera* for Broomhill Opera at Wilton's Music Hall. **TV**: *Princess of Thieves, Poirot, Plain Jane, Doctors* and *Chambers.* **Film**: *Angels and Insects* and *Maybe Baby.*

DANIEL REDMOND
(GOD)
Daniel Redmond trained at University College Bretton Hall, where he graduated with a Drama BA, and at the Royal Academy of Music, Musical Theatre Course. His **theatre** credits include Somal in *La Cava* at the Piccadilly Theatre, Brother Frank in *Seven Brides for Seven Brothers* at BAC, and Ted in *Brighton Beach Scumbags* at the Brockely Jack Theatre.

KATY SECOMBE
(MARY BOLTON)
Katy Secombe trained at Bristol Old Vic Theatre School. Her **theatre** credits include *Guys and Dolls* and *The Winter's Tale* at the National, *Twelfth Night* for NT Education on tour, *Aladdin* and *Cinderella* at the Salisbury Playhouse, *Provocative Acts* and *Peeping at Tom* at the Nuffield, Southampton, *Nervous Breakdown* at the Croydon Warehouse, *Teechers* at Redgrave Theatre, Farnham, *Dick Whittington, The Barber of Seville, The Hostage, Macbeth* and *Blithe Spirit* at Harrogate, *Pickwick* at Chichester Festival Theatre and on tour, *A Christmas Carol* at the Theatre Royal, Nottingham, *The Wiz* at the Hackney Empire, and *Bedroom Farce* at the Stephen Joseph Theatre, Scarborough. **TV**: *Royal Variety Performance, Highway, London's Burning, Olivier Awards, Mega Maths* and *Casualty.*

ALI SICHILONGO
(ENSEMBLE)
Ali Sichilongo trained at Central. His **theatre** credits include *Sparkleshark* for NT Education on tour, *A Time of Fire* at Birmingham Rep and *Six Degrees of Separation* at the Edinburgh Festival, 1999. Ali was an original cast member of *Mother Clap's Molly House* at the National Theatre and is thrilled to be making his West End debut with the production here at the Aldwych Theatre.

JAY SIMPSON
(KEDGER/CHARLIE)
Jay Simpson's **theatre** credits include *Battle Royal* at the National, *Srebrenica* at the Tricycle and the National, *Santa Stole My Giro, Hummingbird* and *Golden Own Goal* at the Old Red Lion, *Afters* at the Old Red Lion, BAC and Edinburgh Festival, *Job Rocking* at Riverside Studios, *Richard III* at the Pleasance and Neuss Shakespeare Festival, and *No Experience Req'd* and *The Good Samaritan* at Hampstead Theatre. **TV**: *Shall I be Mother?, The Baker Street Boys, Nobody Here Knows, The Universe Downstairs, Morning Sarge, Sorry, Relative Strangers, All in Good Faith, Casualty, Press Gang, The Fear, Death of a Son, The Firm, London's Burning, Game On, The Thin Blue Line, Wrestling with the Big One, Thieftakers, A Touch of Frost, Pilgrim's Rest* and *Uncut Funk.* **Film**: *SW9, Erik the Viking, Club Le Monde, This Year's Love, Beautiful People, Someone Else's Dream* and *Three Steps to Heaven.*

DANIELLE TILLEY
(AMY/TINA)
Danielle Tilley trained at LAMDA. Her **theatre** credits include Doll Tearsheet in *Henry IV Part 2* and Phoebe in *As You Like It* for the RSC, *You Be Ted and I'll Be Sylvia* at Hampstead, Miranda in *The Collector* at Derby Playhouse and Royal Lyceum, Edinburgh, *Proposals* at West Yorkshire Playhouse, and the title role in *Educating Rita*, and *Pygmalion* at Wolsey Theatre, Ipswich. **TV** includes *The Student Prince, Dalziel and Pascoe, A Date With..., Island, The Bill, Heartbeat, Peak Practice, The Lodge, The Upper Hand, Home Truths, Palace Hill, Sticks and Stones* and *In the Pink.* **Film**: *Tommy Tough, Beginner's Luck, Boxed In, Washing Day* and *The Window Bed.*

MARK RAVENHILL
(WRITER)

Mark Ravenhill's first full-length play, *Shopping and Fucking*, was produced by Out of Joint and the Royal Court Theatre and opened at the Ambassadors in September 1996 prior to a national tour. It transferred to the Queen's Theatre in the West End in June 1997 prior to an international tour. The play opened in New York in January 1998, and has been produced in Western Australia as well as in foreign-language productions throughout the world. His second play, *Faust is Dead*, was produced by ATC (national tour) in 1997. *Sleeping Around*, a joint venture with three other writers opened in Salisbury in February 1998 before being shown at the Donmar Warehouse, London, followed by a national tour. His play, *Handbag*, was produced by the Actors Touring Company in 1998. His next play, *Some Explicit Polaroids*, for Out of Joint Theatre Co. opened at the New Ambassadors Theatre in October 1999 to great critical acclaim. Mark's new play, *Mother Clap's Molly House*, with music by Matthew Scott, opened at the National Theatre in September 2001 and transferred to the Aldwych Theatre in February 2002. All Mark's plays are published by Methuen Drama Ltd. and have been produced worldwide. **TV** includes *Cab Confessionals* (BBC 2). **Radio** includes *Feed Me* (BBC).

NICHOLAS HYTNER
(DIRECTOR)

Theatre includes *Ghetto*, *The Wind in the Willows*, *The Madness of George III*, *The Recruiting Officer*, *Carousel*, *The Cripple of Inishmaan*, *The Winter's Tale* (National); *Measure for Measure*, *The Tempest*, *King Lear* (RSC). Elsewhere in London, *Miss Saigon* (also Broadway), *Volpone* (Almeida), *The Importance of Being Earnest* (Aldwych), *The Lady in the Van* (Queen's), *Cressida* (Albery), *Orpheus Descending* (Donmar). In New York: *Carousel* and *Twelfth Night* (Lincoln Center). **Opera** includes *The Turn of the Screw*, *King Priam* (Kent Opera), *Rienzi*, *Xerxes*, *The Magic Flute* (ENO), *Don Giovanni* (Munich), *Giulio Cesare*, *The Cunning Little Vixen* (Paris). **Film**: *The Madness of King George*, *The Crucible*, *The Object of My Affection*.

MATTHEW SCOTT
(MUSIC, ORCHESTRATIONS AND MUSICAL DIRECTOR)

Matthew Scott trained at City University and Guildhall, London, at the Kurt Weill Foundation in New York (as Music Assistant to Lotte Lenya), and at the Hochschule fur Musik in Berlin. He has written music for over fifty theatre productions including premieres by Harold Pinter, Nicholas Wright, John Mortimer, Jeremy Sams, Brian Friel and Howard Barker, with whose work he is especially associated as a founder member of the Wrestling School. His work in the West End includes *The Admirable Crichton* and *The Duchess of Malfi*. Other theatre work includes *Volpone* for the RSC, a ballet for London Contemporary Dance Theatre, two full-length plays for marionettes and *Have You Seen This Girl?*, a community opera with libretto by Peter Terson, commissioned and first performed by Broomhill Opera, and he arranged and directed the music for world premieres of Sir Harrison Birtwistle's theatre pieces *The Cat and the Moon* and *The King of the Great Clock Tower*. He has written and directed music for many productions at the National including *The Ticket of Leave Man*, *Animal Farm*, *Fathers and Sons*, *Ting Tang Mine*, *Black Snow*, *The Shoemaker's Holiday*, *Pravda*, *Alice's Adventures Underground* and recent productions of *Private Lives* and *The Heiress*. He has won awards from *Time Out* and the *Evening Standard*.

TV includes *Bedtime*, *Mrs Bradley's Mysteries*, *1900 House*, *Drop the Dead Donkey*, *Underworld*, *Middlemarch*, *Medics* and *In Suspicious Circumstances*. TV films include *The Lord of Misrule*, *Crossing the Floor*, *Eleven Men Against Eleven*, *King Leek*, *Mister White Goes to Westminster* and *Sex and Death*. Films include *The Landgirls*, *The Feast of July*, *Lichtspiel* and *The Whip*. He produced the band TransGlobal Underground in the soundtrack for *King Girl*, was a member of The Lost Jockey, and has performed at many international festivals including Aldeburgh, Vienna, the Venice Biennale and Edinburgh. He is co-author of two books, *Four Bars of Agit* and *The New Orpheus*, winner of the 1983 Deems Taylor Award.

GILES CADLE
(SET DESIGNER)

Giles Cadle studied Architecture at Kingston Polytechnic and Stage Design at Nottingham Polytechnic. He has worked on a large variety of **theatre** and **opera** productions including the set for *She Stoops to Conquer* (directed by Jonathan Miller) for the Gate Theatre, Dublin; set and costumes for *Gangster Number One* (directed by Jonathan Kent) for the Almeida; set and costumes for *Phaedra* (directed by John Crowley); costumes for *Katya Kabanova* (directed by Gale Edwards) for the New Zealand

International Festival Opera. Also set and costumes for a Gate Dublin/Lincoln Center, New York co-production 1996; a presentation of all Beckett's 19 works for the stage, revised for the Beckett Festival at the Barbican in 1999; *Krapp's Last Tape* opened at the New Ambassadors in 2000. In 1997 he designed *Catalpa* for the Gate, Dublin/ Melbourne Festival, which won the Critics' Award as part of the Gate's overall contribution to the 1997 Melbourne Festival. Recent work includes sets for *Midsummer Marriage* for Bayerische Staatsoper, Munich and for *Flight*, a new opera by Jonathan Dove for Glyndebourne Touring Opera both directed by Richard Jones, *Eugene Onegin* for Opera North, *Penelope* at Guildhall and *Svejk* at the Gate, Notting Hill; sets and costumes for *Wrong Mountain* which opened in San Francisco (1999) before transferring to Broadway; *The Beggar's Opera* at the National Opera du Rhin in Strasbourg (2000); and most recently, sets for *The Magic Flute* for English Touring Opera, *Six Characters Looking For an Author* at the Young Vic and *The Shape of Things* for the Almeida. Future projects include *A Midsummer Night's Dream* for the RSC and *The Flying Dutchman* for New York City Opera.

NICKY GILLIBRAND

(COSTUME DESIGNER)

Nicky trained as a fashion textile designer. Current and Recent work: *A Midsummer Night's Dream*, RSC, Dir. Richard Jones; *Hansel and Gretel*, (set and costumes), tour for Opera North, Dir. Tim Supple; *Queen of Spades*, Royal Opera House with Dir. Francesca Zambello, with whom she previously collaborated on *War and Peace*, Paris Opera; *Boris Godunov*, English National Opera and Toronto 2002, and *Lady In the Dark*, Royal National Theatre.

Other productions with Dir. Richard Jones: *Six Characters in Search of an Author*, Young Vic Theatre; *Flight*, Glyndebourne, Nationale Reisopera, Netherlands and Flanders Opera; *Pelleas et Melisande*, Opera North, ENO, Flanders Opera and Munich Festival 2004; *Midsummer Marriage*, Munich; *Mazeppa*, indoor Bregenzer Festspiele; *Le Bourgeois Gentilhomme*, Royal National Theatre. Previously: *Turk in Italy* and *La Gioconda* as part of the Autumn 2000 Italian Season for English National Opera; *Peter Grimes* with Tim Albery; *La Lupa* for the Royal Shakespeare Company with Dir. Simona Gonella at the

Other Place and Barbican Theatre; *La Traviata* (set and costumes), Dir. Annabel Arden; *Don Carlos; Wozzeck; Don Giovanni; Of Thee I Sing* and *Love Life* all for Opera North; *Little Night Music*, RNT, Dir. Sean Mathias. **Film** includes *Institute Benjamenta* with the Brothers Quay.

RICK FISHER

(LIGHTING DESIGNER)

Originally from the USA, Rick Fisher is currently Chairman of the British Association of Lighting Designers, and is also Visiting Professor in Lighting Design at the Dramatisk Institut, Stockholm. Amongst his numerous productions for the Royal National Theatre, he has won Olivier Awards for Best Lighting Design for *Lady in the Dark* and *Chips with Everything* (1998), and *Machinal* (1994). He also won the Tony and Drama Desk awards for the National's production of *An Inspector Calls*, currently at the Playhouse. Other productions at the National include *The Winter's Tale, Blue/Orange, Albert Speer, Widowers' Houses, Betrayal, Flight, Death of a Salesman, Blinded by the Sun, Under Milk Wood* and *Fair Ladies At a Game of Poem Cards*. Other recent work has included, in the West End, *Star Quality* (Apollo), *Afore Night Come* (Young Vic), *Boston Marriage, My Zinc Bed, Far Away, Napoleon, Miss Julie, Lenny, The Hunchback of Notre Dame* for Disney in Berlin, and *A Russian in the Woods* for the RSC, and *Lear* for the Globe in Tokyo. **Opera** includes *Of Mice and Men* in Washington, *Egyptian Helen* and *Wozzeck* for Sante Fe Opera, Verdi's *Requiem, Der Freischutz, Dr Ox's Experiment* and *The Fairy Queen* for ENO, *Wozzeck* in Florence, *Flying Dutchman* in Bordeaux, *La Traviata* for Paris Opera, *Gloriana, Medea* and *La Bohème* for Opera North. **Dance** includes *Cinderella* and *Swan Lake* for Adventure in Motion Pictures.

JANE GIBSON

(DIRECTOR OF MOVEMENT)

Jane Gibson is Head of Movement at the Royal National Theatre and her credits include: *Fuente Ovejuna, Hamlet, Ghetto, Peer Gynt, The Crucible, Richard III, Piano, The Wind in the Willows, Black Snow, Angels in America, Uncle Vanya, Pygmalion, The Rise and Fall of Little Voice, A Midsummer Night's Dream, Macbeth, Arcadia, Sweeney Todd, Mountain Giants, Broken Glass, Volpone, The Prince's Play, Blue Remembered Hills, The Day I Stood Still, An Enemy of the People, Peter*

Pan, Flight, Money, Battle Royal, The Villains' Opera, Romeo and Juliet, The Cherry Orchard and The Cherry Orchard, D. Lindsay Posner. For the RSC credits include: The Revenger's Tragedy, The Plain Dealer, Don Juan, Elgar's Rondo, School for Scandal, The Rivals and Twelfth Night. Her credits in **opera** include: La Traviata, Julius Caesar and Gawain (Royal Opera House), La Clemenza di Tito (Glyndebourne), The Force of Destiny and Mahagonny (ENO), The Rake's Progress (Welsh National Opera), The Marriage of Figaro (Aix en Provence) and Falstaff (Salzburg). She is an Associate Director of Cheek by Jowl. **TV** includes Tom Jones, Far From the Madding Crowd, Great Expectations, Emma, Pride and Prejudice (for which she received an Emmy nomination), Madame Bovary, Wives and Daughters, The Scarlet Pimpernel, The Russian Bride, Love in a Cold Climate and Night Song. Films include Cousin Bette, Firelight, Sense and Sensibility, Mansfield Park, Kate and Leopold and Iris.

NEIL ALEXANDER
(SOUND DESIGNER)
Neil Alexander's recent designs include All My Sons (sound re-creation), Marriage Play/Finding the Sun, Remembrance of Things Past, The Waiting Room, Blue Orange and Sparkleshark. For the Royal Court: Yard Gal, Been So Long, Fair Game, Bailegangaire, Heredity, Penetrator. Other design credits include Two Horsemen (Gate/Bush), The Snake House (Greenwich), The Year of the Family (Finborough).

COLIN PINK
(SOUND DESIGNER)
Colin Pink trained at Guildhall. After working as a Sound Designer in a number of regional rep' theatres he joined the National where he has designed shows including Rosencrantz and Guildenstern are Dead, The London Cuckolds, Troilus and Cressida, Honk! The Ugly Duckling, The Villains' Opera, House/Garden and The Relapse. He was associate designer on My Fair Lady and principal operator on Guys and Dolls, Lady in the Dark, Oklahoma! and Candide.

PATSY RODENBURG
(COMPANY VOICE WORK)
Patsy Rodenburg trained at the Central School of Speech and Drama. She is Head of Voice at the Royal National Theatre and Guildhall School of Music and Drama, and was voice tutor at the Royal Shakespeare Company for nine years. She works extensively in theatre, film, TV and radio throughout Europe, North America, Australia and Asia. She has given lessons to many of the world's leading theatre and opera companies, and maintains a continuous working relationship with Stratford Festival Theatre (Canada), Shared Experience, Cheek by Jowl, Theatre de Complicite, Method and Madness, the Almeida Theatre, the Donmar Warehouse, the Royal Court Theatre, and Michael Howard Studio, New York. She is a Director of the Voice and Speech Centre, London. Publications: The Right to Speak, The Need for Words and The Actor Speaks, all published by Methuen. Video: A Voice of Your Own. Audio tape: The Right to Speak.

CRISPIN BONHAM CARTER
(STAFF DIRECTOR)
Crispin Bonham Carter is an actor and director. With his New Action Theatre he has directed Gamblers by Nicolai Gogol and Four Dogs and a Bone by John Patrick Shanley. He was recently awarded the Jerwood Young Director's Bursary and will be directing performances of new writing as part of the Old Vic New Voices season. As an actor, his **TV** credits include Absolutely Fabulous, Murder Rooms, Victoria and Albert, Wuthering Heights, Game On, Pride and Prejudice, Scarlet and Black and Full Throttle. **Theatre** includes Charley's Aunt at the Sheffield Crucible, Major Barbara and Le Misanthrope for the Peter Hall Co., Gogol's Diary of a Madman at the Finborough, and he has narrated Peter and the Wolf for the English Chamber Orchestra. **Film** includes Bridget Jones' Diary and Howards End.

Trial of Thomas Wright, for Sodomy, April 1726

Evidence of William Davison: The discovering of the Molly Houses was chiefly owing to a quarrel betwixt P——— and ——— Harrington; for upon this quarrel, P———, to be revenged on Harrington, had blabbed something of the secret, and afterwards gave a large information. The Mollies had heard a little of the first discovery, but did not imagine how far he had proceeded, and what farther designs he had upon them. By his means, I and Davison were introduced to the Company, at the prisoner's lodgings. In a large room there we found one a-fiddling and eight more a-dancing country dances, making vile motions, and singing, *Come let us fuck finely*. Then they sat in one another's lap, talked bawdy, and practised a great many indecencies. There was a door in the great room, which opened into a little room, where there was a bed, and into this little room several of the company went; sometimes they shut the door after them, but sometimes they left it open, and then we could see part of their actions. The prisoner was very fond of us, and kissed us all at parting in a very lewd manner.

Trial of Margaret Clap, for keeping a Sodomitical House, July 1726

Evidence of Samuel Stevens: On Sunday night, the 14th of November last, I went to the prisoner's house in Field Lane, in Holborn, where I found between 40 and 50 men making love to one another, as they called it. Sometimes they would sit in one another's laps, kissing in a lewd manner and using their hand indecently. Then they would get up, dance and make curtsies, and mimic the voices of women. O, Fie Sir! ——Pray, Sir, —— Dear, Sir, —— Lord, how can you serve me so? —— I swear I'll cry out. —— You're a wicked Devil, —— and you've a bold face. —— Eh! ye little dear Toad! Come, buss! —— Then they'd hug, and play, and toy, and go out by couples into another room on the same floor, to be married as they called it. The door of that room was kept by ——— Ecclestone, who used to stand pimp for 'em, to prevent anybody from disturbing them in their diversions. When they came out, they used to brag, in plain terms, of what they had been doing. As for the prisoner, she was present all the time, except when she went out to fetch liquors.

Trial of William Brown, for Sodomitical Practices, July 1726

Evidence of Thomas Newton: There's a walk in the Upper-Moor-Fields, by the side of the wall that parts the Upper-Field from the Middle-Field. I knew that this walk was frequented by sodomites, and was no stranger to the methods they used in picking one another up. So I takes a turn that way, and leans over the wall. In a little time the prisoner passes by, and looks hard at me, and, at a small distance from me, stands up against the wall, as if he was going to make water. Then by degrees he sidles nearer and nearer to where I stood, 'till at last he comes close to me. —— *'Tis a very fine night, says he; Aye, says I, and so it is.* Then he takes me by the hand, and after squeezing and playing with it a little (to which I showed no dislike) he conveys it to his breeches.

Extracts taken from trials at the Sessions House in the Old Bailey

background

background produced the twentieth anniversary revival of Julian Mitchell's *Another Country*, which reopened the Arts Theatre in 2000 and Caryl Churchill's *Top Girls* (Aldwych Theatre and national tours, a co-production with the Oxford Stage Company). Other productions this spring include the Cameron Mackintosh production of *Five Guys Named Moe* (UK tour, February to July), Kenneth Lonergan's *This is Our Youth* and Ariel Dorfman's new play, *Purgatory*.

Since 1998 **background** has specialised in theatre production and general management. The company has worked with regional producing houses, touring companies, independent producers and international promoters, on over 80 projects, in the West End, across the UK and abroad. Among others **background** has worked with: The Abbey Theatre Dublin, The Arts Theatre, Birmingham Rep, Concentric Circles, The David Glass Ensemble, Fiery Angel, The Old Vic, Out of the Blue, Out of Joint, The Royal National Theatre, Sadler's Wells, Sphinx, Theatre Royal Bath and The Young Vic. Productions include: *Arabian Nights, The BFG, Carmen, Cherished Disappointments in Love, Drummers, Dolly West's Kitchen, Five Kinds of Silence, Hinterland, Our Country's Good, Feelgood, Phaedra, Rita, Sue and Bob Too, Single Spies, Sliding with Suzanne, The Snowman, So Long Life, Some Explicit Polaroids, A State Affair* and *The 39 Steps*.

background also operates a production resource facility, providing both staff and equipment for all scales of arts production. In February, **background** opens 36 Soho Square, a magnificent seventeenth-century town house, which will provide office, meeting and entertaining space for the arts, media and creative decision makers.

For **background**

Director	**Phil Cameron**
General Manager	**Michael Robey**
Marketing Manager	**Margred Price**
Finance Manager	**Kulwinder Kaur**
Finance Assistant	**Mark Moss-Bowpitt**
Administrator	**Liz Reynolds**
Administrative Assistants	**Carolyn Facer**
	Georgina Harper
Head of Technical & Production	**Sacha Milroy**
Technical & Production Co-ordinator	**Ben Turner**
Production Assistant	**Kate Lavender**
Production Managers	**Paul Hennessy**
	Dave Ferrier
Technical Managers	**Gareth Baston**
	Steve Bush
	Tim Mascall
	Koen van Geene
Company Manager	**Rosie Gilbert**
Assistant Resources Manager	**Kevin McDermott**
Manager, 36 Soho Square	**Frazer Hoyle**

For **Mother Clap's Molly House**

Press	**Bridget Thornborrow**
	(020 7247 4437)
Advertising, Marketing & Design	**Dewynters plc**
	(020 7321 0488)
Production Sound	**Orbital Sound Ltd.**
Production Electrics/Lighting	**Sparks Theatrical Hire Ltd.**
Production Insurance	**Walton & Parkinson**
Production Transport	**Southern Van Lines**
Musical Orchestration	**Matthew Scott**
Engineering	**WeldFab Engineering Ltd.**
Carpentry	**Terry Murphy**
Scenery	**Scott Fleary Ltd**
A-Z painting	**Scanachrome**
Cloths	**Gerriets UK & Ken Creasy Ltd.**
Programme research	**Lyn Haill & Dinah Wood**

A-Z map reproduced by permission of Geographers' A-Z Map Co Ltd.
This product includes mapping data licensed from Ordnance Survey ®.
© Crown Copyright 2000. License number 1200017302.

The National's workshops are responsible for, on this production:
Armoury; Costume; Props & furniture; Scenic construction;
Scenic painting; Wigs

NT Royal National Theatre

Mother Clap's Molly House had its world premiere at the National Theatre, where the production played in repertoire from September 2001. Within the National are three separate theatres, the Olivier, the Lyttelton (where *Mother Clap's Molly House* was seen); and the Cottesloe.

The chief aims of the National, under the direction of Trevor Nunn, are to present a diverse repertoire, embracing classic, new and neglected plays; to present these plays to the very highest standards; and to give audiences a wide choice.

We offer all kinds of other events and services—short early-evening platform performances; work for children and education work; free live entertainment both inside and outdoors at holiday times; exhibitions; live foyer music; backstage tours; bookshops; plenty of places to eat and drink; and easy car-parking. And the nearby Studio acts as a resource for research and development for actors, writers and directors. We send productions on tour, both in this country and abroad, and do all we can, through ticket-pricing, to make the NT accessible to everyone regardless of income.

In the Olivier till the end of April you can see Trevor Nunn's new production of Rodgers & Hammerstein's *South Pacific*, which will be followed by Peter Hall's production of Euripides' *Bacchai*, and a trilogy of new plays by Tom Stoppard. In the Lyttelton, Harold Pinter's enigmatic masterpiece *No Man's Land*, directed by the author, plays in repertoire with the National Theatre of Brent's "tasteful yet shocking exposé" *The Wonder of Sex*, followed by Martin Clunes as Molière's *Tartuffe*, in a new version by Ranjit Bolt. Coming up in the Cottesloe are Pamela Gien's acclaimed performance of her own play *The Syringa Tree*, from New York, and Sebastian Barry's new play *Hinterland*

The National beyond the South Bank: Charlotte Jones' *Humble Boy* is at the Gielgud; Michael Frayn's *Noises Off* is at the Piccadilly and also in New York; *An Inspector Calls* at the Playhouse; and *The Island* visits the Old Vic for a limited season; Trevor Nunn's production of *Oklahoma!* is at the Gershwin Theatre on Broadway from 21 March (previews from 23 February). On tour are *The Good Hope*, *No Man's Land*, *Life x 3* and *Copenhagen*.

Box Office: 020-7452 3000
Registered Charity No. 224223

Chairman of the Board	Sir Christopher Hogg
Director of the Royal National Theatre	Trevor Nunn
Director Designate	Nicholas Hytner
Executive Director	Genista McIntosh
Head of Touring	Roger Chapman

Orme: **Lord intended each of us to have a father and a mother and if Nature don't provide 'em, we must do what we can.**

Mother Clap's Molly House, **Act I, scene iii**

There is scarcely any less bother in the running of a family than in that of an entire state. And domestic business is no less importunate for being less important.

MONTAIGNE, *ESSAIS*, 1580-88

I was ever of the opinion that the honest man who married and brought up a large family did more service than he who continued single and only talked of population.

OLIVER GOLDSMITH, *THE VICAR OF WAKEFIELD*, 1761-2, PUBLISHED 1766

Assume a particular state of development in the productive facilities of man and you will get a particular form of commerce and consumption. Assume particular stages of development in production, commerce and consumption and you will have a corresponding social constitution, a corresponding organisation of the family, of orders or of classes, in a word, a corresponding civil society. Assume a particular civil society and you will get particular political conditions which are only the official expression of civil society.

KARL MARX, LETTER TO PV ANNENKOV, 1846

Accidents will occur in the best-regulated families; and in families not regulated by that pervading influence which sanctifies while it enhances the – a – I would say, in short, by the influence of Woman, in the lofty character of Wife, they may be expected with confidence, and must be borne with philosophy.

CHARLES DICKENS, *DAVID COPPERFIELD* (MR MICAWBER), 1849-50

I can trace my ancestry back to a protoplasmal primordial atomic globule. Consequently, my family pride is something in-conceivable. I can't help it. I was born sneering.

WS GILBERT, *THE MIKADO*, 1881

Good families are generally worse than any others.

ANTHONY HOPE, *THE PRISONER OF ZENDA*, 1894

Families! I hate you! Enclosed hallways, shut doors, jealous possessions of happiness.

ANDRÉ GIDE, *LES NOURRITURES TERRESTRES*, 1897

I believe that more unhappiness comes from this source than any other – I mean from the attempt to prolong family connection unduly and to make people hang together artificially who would never naturally do so. The mischief among the lower classes is not so great, but among the middle and upper classes it is killing a large number daily. And the old people do not really like it much better than the young.

SAMUEL BUTLER (1835-1902), *FURTHER EXTRACTS FROM THE NOTE BOOKS*, 1934

Mother Clap's Molly House

Mother Clap's Molly House was developed with the following students at LAMDA (London Academy of Music and Dramatic Arts): James Adams, Samuel Barnett, Jack Bennet, Kieran Brew, Nicholas Burns, Louise J. Cox, Gus Danowski, Daniella Dessa, Henry Douthwaite, Felicite de Jeu, Will Huggins, Lisa Jackson, Marie Lewis, Daniel Llewlyn-Williams, Anna Maxwell-Martin, Tom McKay, Jamie Michie, Gavin Molloy, Claire Redcliffe, Francesca Rogers, Gary Shelford, Stephanie Street, David Sturzaker, Rebecca Todd, Leatsa Tsimbris and Aaron Woodman.

Thanks to Peter James, Cat Horn and everyone at LAMDA

Mother Clap's Molly House was first performed at the Lyttelton Theatre, Royal National Theatre, on 24 August 2001. The cast was as follows:

Mrs Tull	Deborah Findlay
Stephen Tull	Iain Mitchell
Martin, *their apprentice*	Paul Ready
Princess Seraphina	Ian Redford

Whores

Amelia	Maggie McCarthy
Amy	Danielle Tilley
Mary Cranton	Debbie Chazen
Mary Bolton	Katy Secombe

Working Men

Kedger	Jay Simpson
Philips	William Osborne
Thomas Orme, *their apprentice*	Dominic Cooper
Gabriel Lawrence	Con O'Neill

Deities

God	Daniel Redmond
Eros	Paul J. Medford

Josh	Dominic Cooper
Will	William Osborne
Charlie	Jay Simpson
Tina	Danielle Tilley
Tom	Paul Ready
Edward	Iain Mitchell
Phil	Con O'Neill

Other parts played by: Deborah Asante, Martin
Chamberlain, Pamela Hardman, Luke Jardine, Tom
McKay, Iain Pearson, Philip Ralph, Ali Sichilongo

Director Nicholas Hytner
Set Designer Giles Cadle
Costume Designer Nicky Gillibrand
Lighting Designer Rick Fisher
Music Director Paul Frankish
Director of Movement Jane Gibson
Sound Designers Neil Alexander, Colin Pink
Company Voice Work Patsy Rodenburg

A slash in the dialogue (/) indicates the cue for the next
actor to start speaking, creating overlapping dialogue

Act One

'Opening Act One'

Scene One

Chorus

When at first Our Father mighty
Made the Earth and Sea and Skies
Then Our Father great and mighty
Made Man and gave him Enterprise.

God

Enterprise, shall make you human
Getting, spending – spark divine
This my gift to you poor human:
Purse celestial, coin divine.

London is revealed – a city of business and enterprise.

All

Enterprise, come light our darkness
Business, shape our heart and hand!
Then – oh rich Our Father mighty! –
Lead us to the promised land.

London vanishes to reveal:

Tally shop. A large number of dresses. Workbench.

Mrs Tull *at the counter. Enter* **Martin**.

Martin   Sorry I took so long only I –

Tull   Martin. Where you been?

Martin   Get thread like Master said only I –

Tull   Get thread? Get thread? Dun't take hour and more
to get thread.

Martin   Well, see, I was gonna go up –

Tull   Weren't just thread, ask me. Weren't just errand.
You was wandering again, wun't you?

Martin   No. No.

Tull   Thought so. Wandering. How many times Master
told you: Boy, dun't you wander or you'll feel my fist?

Martin   I know but I wun't –

Tull   If there's one thing he hates most in the world it's
apprentice boy who wanders. Where you go, Martin?

Martin   I dunno. I get lost easy.

Tull   Cos we worry when you in't back, see? See you
might think: man, look after meself. But we think: boy.

Martin   Yes, Mrs Tull.

Tull   There's Mother and Father to keep a boy straying
from the path and we in't Mother and Father but still
there's a worry when you're off.

Martin   Yes, Mrs Tull. Master awful angry?

Tull   No. Master's . . .

Martin   He had a fit?

Tull   No. Just . . . Master's took peculiar. And Master's
resting hisself. So I'm out the front today.

Martin   What? You? You're gonna – ?

Tull   Thass right. I'm gonna drive the bargains. I'm gonna
write them in the book. I'm gonna . . .

Martin   Yeah?

Tull   Oh, Martin. Figures is hard, in't they? You make
anything of that?

Tull *shows* **Martin** *the ledger.*

Martin   No.

Tull   In't numbers terrible things? Dance around when I look at them.

Martin   He shoulda taught you.

Tull   No. See I'm Wife. And ledger's – well, he's always done ledger. But now –

Martin   So what you gonna do when customer arrives and there's writing in to do?

Tull   I dun't know. Muddle through. Don't you worry about me. I'll find a way. Now you. Out the back. Great deal of mending to do today. Them two whores we hired to yesterday got into an awful fight on account of them both going after the same customer – him being the only customer a-loitering in Covent Garden – and ripped the dresses awful. So you put that thread to good use.

Martin   Yes, Mrs Tull.

Martin *goes to exit.*

Tull   Martin –

Martin   Yes, Mrs Tull?

Tull   Nothing. Just . . .

Martin   You frightened?

Tull   Frightened? No. Watched him often enough, in I? Show the sluts the dresses. Bargain with the sluts. Write the sluts' money in the book. Can't be so hard, can it?

Martin   No. Can't be so hard.

Tull   Wish me luck?

Martin   Good luck.

Exit **Martin**.

Pause. The shop bell rings. Enter **Princess Seraphina** *– a large man in a dress.*

Princess   Hello. Hello. Howdeedo.

Tull   . . .

Princess   Looking for your husband.

Tull   . . .

Princess   I'm looking for work.

Tull   . . .

Princess   See. I have a good hand.

He picks up a garment.

This one's been hurried. Poor thread in a poor light I should say. And if you're working with poor thread in a poor light you gotta have great skill otherwise – Now this (*his own dress*) is my own work. Now you look at the way the lace meets the body here. Perfect match. And you compare that work (*the dress from* **Tull**'s *shop*) to this. No comparison. Heaven and Earth. Shit and silver. Come run your hand over it. See.

He takes **Tull**'s *hand and runs it over his dress.*

What do you think of that?

Tull   What are you?

Princess   Princess Seraphina. Howdeedo.

Tull   You're a man.

Princess   Thass right.

Tull   In a dress.

Princess   Thass right.

Tull (*calls*)   Stephen. Stephen. It's a man. In a dress.

Enter **Stephen** *at great speed.*

Stephen   Told you: no work here.

Princess   But my rates are fair.

Stephen   I'll call the watch.

Princess   No rates fairer than mine. No work better than mine.

Stephen   Then let some sodomite take you on. Let 'em look to their own.

Princess   I'm not a sodomite.

Stephen   Or molly or mary or ingle. Whatever you are.

Princess   No, no. I'm a man as ever you are.

Stephen   Listen to it. Man. Rigged up like that.

Princess (*to* **Tull**)   See, when I'm dressed in trousers I get awful vicious. I think the whole world's against me and I strike out with my fists. But in a dress –

Stephen   I don't want – no.

Stephen *staggers*.

Tull   Oh, love.

Princess   Please, I gotta eat. Not asking for charity. I'm a good worker.

Stephen   Agh. Burning. Agh.

Tull (*to* **Princess**)   You're gonna kill him.

Stephen   Agh.

Tull (*to* **Stephen**)   Sit yourself down. Thass it.

Stephen   Aaaaagggh.

Tull   You got no right. Come in here trying to kill him. (*To* **Stephen**.) Thass it love. Hold on. I'm here. I'm here for you. (*To* **Princess**.) You be on your way.

Princess   I'm only asking –

Tull   And I'm saying: no. See – good Lord made two natures. Him. Thass man. And then – bit of his rib – woman. Thass me. There in't no room for third sex. You're against Nature. No wonder he got burning in the head.

Princess   That in't me. Oh no.

Tull   Oh yes.

Princess   Burning in the head? In't me. Burning in the
head? Thass pox. On account of all the sluts he's fucked,
that is.

Tull   No no no. I in't listening. Go go go. You mincing
dog. You swivelling no-prick. Out. Out.

She pushes **Princess** *out of the shop.*

Tull   Oh, Stephen. In't it a wicked creature? Wicked
creature saying evil words.

Stephen   You did well there, me love, see him off. You're
gotta be strong once I'm carried off.

Tull   No. That in't gonna –

Stephen   Oh yes. Wun't be long before I'm dead as dead.

Tull   No, love.

Stephen   More fits 'an ever now. Burning in me head
night and day.

Tull   No – good Lord in't gonna carry off man of industry,
man of business. It's the makers, it's the savers, it's the
spenders and traders who are most blessed. In't no love like
the Lord's love of business. Thass what you said.

Stephen   Listen. He's taking me cos . . . He's taking me
cos I'm bad.

Tull   No. Good man.

Stephen   See, he loves business, what he dun't love is . . .
lustful thoughts.

Tull   You in't had lustful thoughts, Stephen.

Stephen   Oh yes, my love. Multitudes of 'em. Night and
day.

Tull   Then thass me to blame. Thass woman tempting you.

Stephen   No, me love, in't you. And I've done lustful deeds.

Tull   No, no.

Stephen   Oh, how can you be so blind? You must have seen –

Tull   Seen nothing.

Stephen   You must have heard.

Tull   Heard nothing.

Stephen   In't you even wondered? When I in't . . . took you for twenty years.

Tull   Thass the way with marriage. First year is always nothing but lovemaking, after that – blue moon. Any Old Wife'll tell you that.

Stephen   See – there's God of industry, yes. And he smiles on London now. Gonna make us greatest city in the world. But then there's – oh, love, I got Eros whispering in me ear all the day long.

Tull   Then you gotta fight him.

Stephen   And I try. God says: Make money. But Eros says –

Tull   You wanna buss a little love? You wanna take me? That what you want? Come. I know it in't much of a body but I'm willing. I'm yours, love, you must do with me as you will.

Tull *pulls up her skirts.*

Stephen   There's been others.

Tull   No.

Stephen   There's been hundreds of others.

Tull   What's that? Can't hear you.

Stephen   All the day long. Ledger? Ledger's a lie. There's been monies out to buy whores, monies out for trinkets for my sluts, there's been drinking and gambling with doxies, there's – That's why we in't got new stock. Thass why you're always mending. That's why we got so few customers.

Tull (*sings unaccompanied during the above*)
    Our rates are fair
    So climb the stair
    To Tull's, to Tull's, to Tull's.

Stephen   Listen to me. I'm gonna be struck down! I'm gonna die! I'm gonna burn for ever! One more lustful thought and I'm gone!

Bell rings. Enter **Amelia** *and* **Amy**.

Amelia   Well, will you look at this. New stock! (**Amy**) Thank fuck the good Lord has smiled on me at last. I'd almost given up hope. All the old stock's fucked and the only customers we see is a Lord who wants a whipping once a week and a Critic of Plays who promises to pay another day. And how's a whorehouse to thrive on that? But now this – oh, won't they come from miles around to fuck this?

Tull   Stephen –

Stephen   That's it, love. See to the customers.

Amelia   Every day I've been waiting for those bloody coaches to arrive from the country – and out they step – lame girls, starved girls, girls with fingers missing, girls with hair on their chins and breath like a fart – and then: out she steps. Come to Mother I say and here we are. Now then – Shepherdess for this one.

Amy   I never cared for sheep. Family's been shepherds for years. But – used to hear them bells ringing round them bloody beasts' necks and I'd think: fuck you. Wun't have to live like this much longer. It's the bells of London for me.

Amelia   Thass right. Gonna make your fortune in London.

Amy   Fortune? Dun't know about that. Fair amount, I reckon. Got a clean body, willing manner.

Amelia   Do you have a shepherdess?

Tull   Don't know. Stephen –

Stephen   Measure her first.

Amy   Mother always made my clothes.

Amelia   Well, I'm Mother now.

Tull   You miss her?

Amy   Oh no. I never cared for her. Shepherd's wife. Thass a stupid thing to be, isn't it?

Tull   She'll miss you.

Amy   Oh no. Fourteen children. One less'd be a blessed relief I should say. Though I was always the fairest.

Tull   Is that so?

Amy   Oh yes. They'd all say – from preacher to pigman – 'by God, that's a fair child' and they'd try for a fumble but I thought: no. For I shall be a whore in London and make my money and ride through here in a carriage and gob on you.

Amelia   Maidenhead too? Oh Lord, in't He smiling down on me today. Got a Sir Somebody willing to pay twenty guineas to feel a hymen snap and see the blood come.

Amy   Twenty guineas? Fuck me. Twenty guineas. In't it a marvel what a body's worth?

Tull   Is this the manner of thing you had in mind?

Amelia   No. I want higher on the leg, a cap, a crook.

Tull   Might have something out the back. If you wanna – (*To* **Amelia**.) He had a turn, gotta rest himself.

Exit **Tull** *and* **Amelia**. *Pause.*

Amy   Well, I better . . .

She starts to take off her dress.

You ever been to the country?

Stephen   No.

Amy   Country's alright for a child. But then I grew, see?

Stephen   Yes?

Amy   Do you think I'll make a good whore?

Stephen   Don't know.

Amy   Don't you think I'm fair?

Stephen   Fair enough.

Amy   In't that a wonder? Twenty guineas take a maidenhead. Shall we look at it?

Stephen   At . . . ?

Amy   Oh, fetch a mirror and let's look at my little marvel.

Stephen   No.

Amy   Oh, here.

She has found a little hand mirror. She puts it on the floor. She pulls her skirts up to her knees and stands over the mirror.

Now open up and . . . no. Can't see it yet. I shall need you to hold the mirror higher. Here.

Amy *holds the mirror out to* **Stephen**.

Stephen   No. Can't.

Amy   Oh please, sir. You gotta help me. It's a grand day when a girl finds her body in't just eating and shitting, in't it? Day when a girl discovers she's a commodity.

Stephen   But there's lustful thoughts.

Amy   Oh no. Ain't no lust in a whore. Just business. Thass why God smiles on 'em.

Stephen   My lustful thoughts.

Amy   In't much lust in just looking, is there? I shan't let you touch. Come.

She hands **Stephen** *the mirror. She sits on the counter, pulls up her skirts, opens her legs.*

Now, sir, look into me.

Reluctantly, **Stephen** *does so.*

See hymen?

Stephen   I don't . . . reckon maybe . . . .

Amy   Now mirror up and let's marvel at Katie Cunt together.

Enter **Tull**, **Amelia** *and* **Martin**. **Amelia** *carries a shepherdess dress.*

Amelia   Now isn't this just the thing? Quick, miss. Don't delay.

Amelia *and* **Amy** *exit to put on the dress.* **Stephen** *sees* **Martin**.

Stephen   Oh, back at last, are you? Wanderer returns. Well, I hope you give him sharp words. You spoil him with soft tongue. Can't make him your infant.

Tull   Yes, Stephen.

Stephen   Oh, wife, I know you wanted an infant.

Tull   Oh yes. We both wanted that. Infants.

Stephen   Hundreds of 'em, eh?

Tull   Hundreds? Oh. That'd wear a body out.

Stephen   Dozens of 'em. Calling out night and day. Mum Mum Mum.

Tull   Dad Dad Dad

Stephen   And that never happened but –

Tull   Oh, I wanted to hold on to 'em. Wanted that more than all the world. Just my body never could.

Stephen   Don't fret yourself, love.

Tull   Heart said kid. Head said kid. Just Body could never hold on for more 'an a month.

Enter **Amelia** *and* **Amy** *in the shepherdess outfit.*

Amy   Oh, dun't I look wonderful? They'll all be standing to attention when I walks past.

Amelia   At last. Back in business.

Stephen *clutches at his head.*

Amy (*recites*)
   Lost sir lost sir searching high and low
   Looking for my sheep sir – oh where did they go?
   Oh pity me, oh pity me – a poor simple Jill
   Who only wants a flock sir
   To drive up her hill.

Stephen   Aaagh.

Amelia   I'll hire a boy. Run through the streets crying: Best fuck in London.

Stephen   Oh. Lust. Lust.

Tull   You gotta fight it, Stephen.

Amy   Oh yes. I'm the one they all want a fuck. Look at me. Look at my bubbies. Rise and fall. Rise and fall.

Stephen   Oh, love. Lord's gonna strike me down.

Tull   Think of ledgers, Stephen. Think of monies in. Monies out. Balance. Surplus.

Amy   There never was a girl like me. Oh, in't I wonderful?

Amelia   He'll cry: Come and fuck her each and everyone.

Tull   Figures. Numbers. Stock.

Amy   Cunt. Cunt. Cunt. In't I got a wonderful cunt?

Stephen   Aaaagggghhhh.

Tull   Don't let it into your head.

Amy   Look up me. Come into me. Work away. Make me whole.

Amelia   Good Lord, for what you have sent me – thank you, thank you.

Amy   Oh, the smell of me. Oh, the taste of me.

Tull *grabs the ledger – holds it up in front of* **Stephen**.

Tull   Numbers. Add 'em up. Total 'em. Carry 'em forward.

Stephen   Can't see 'em. Dancing.

Amy   How do you want me? Forwards? Backwards? Bring your friends, bring your family, cos Amy's here.

Stephen   Aaagggh.

Tull *flies at* **Amy**, *hitting her with the ledger*.

Tull   Stop that, miss. Just you – stop that.

Amelia   Mind my stock. Don't damage the goods.

Tull   Cover your mouth, girl. That's evil. That's muck.

Amy   Old woman. You're dry. I'm wet. In't that right, sir? I'm moist. (*To* **Martin**.) Come on, boy, you want me? Oh, there's me flock. Baaa! Baaa! Baaa! Come, ram – tup away. Baaaa!

Stephen   Aaaaghh. Lord's coming for me now.

Tull   No. Stephen. Stay. Stay.

Stephen   Can't hold out much longer. Aaaaagggh!

Tull   You gotta live, love.

Stephen   Aaagggh. Quick – you gotta listen. Running the business. So much to tell you. Quick. Aaaagh. Lessons to give you.

Stephen *collapses.*

Tull   Stephen – no.

Stephen   Ledger's yours now, love. Shop's yours. Aaaaggggh.

Tull   But, Stephen, I don't know how. Stephen, I can't.

Stephen   Aaaaggggh.

Stephen*'s body convulses several times and is then still. Pause.*

Tull   Come on, love. You gotta come and teach me, love. Love. Can't go 'til I'm ready. Not ready to be alone. Love. Love. I'm here for you, love. Stephen. Stop that. You're a good man. Oh Lord.

Pause.

Amy   It weren't me, was it?

Scene Two

'Funeral, Motto 2 and Wake'

Chorus
    The Widow's in a sorry state
    With Husband dead and gone
    But tears won't bring back
    Milk that's spilt
    And *The Widow Carries On.*

The tally shop. A wake. **Stephen Tull***'s body lies in an open coffin. A large number of people – men and women – among them the whores – including* **Amelia**, **Amy**, **Cranton** *and* **Bolton**. **Amy** *is still in the shepherdess outfit. They've all been drinking heavily for some* *time. A couple of musicians play. People are dancing drunkenly. Enter* **Martin**.

Martin   Ho there. Ho there.

Music stops.

Widow says: Thank you for coming. But now she's took to her bed.

Amelia   Oh no, that isn't right.

Martin   Took to her bed and she in't coming out.

Amelia   Widow's gotta join the wake.

Mourners agree.

Martin   Thass what she says and she says: Go home now.

Amelia   What? Quick jig and a mug of ale and off we go. Oh no. Dance 'til you drop. Drink 'til you reel. More beer –

Martin   No. You gotta go.

Bolton   Beer, boy, beer.

Martin   There in't no more.

Amelia   And strike up there.

The band starts 'Wake 2', but **Martin** *shouts them down.*

Martin   No!

The band stops.

Bolton   Bit of pleasure. Thass all we want.

Cranton   Shit old life. Wake comes along, you gotta make the most of it.

Bolton   You wanna enjoy yourself, boy. Tally shop in't gonna last long, you ask me.

Martin   Oh no. Carrying on. You'll see.

Cranton   You wanna look for a new trade, boy. Less you wanna starve. Who's got a head for business? Not her. Not you.

Amelia   Come on, boy. Dance while you can. Music!

The band plays 'Wake 3', the mourners dance. Finally, **Tull** *enters.*

Tull   Thass enough now. Time to go. Finished now.

Silence.

See, it's just me and him now. Thass proper way to send him off. Always said to me: 'My love, the rest of the world is either customers or thieves. And as long as we make sure the customers fill our purse and the thieves dun't snatch it, then what do we care for them? The world is you and me and there's an end to it.' So just you leave us be. I got a lot I want to ask him.

Amelia   D'you think he'll answer?

Tull   He'll find a way. Wun't you, love?

Amelia   D'you think you could ask him about new stock for the shop?

Tull   Oh no, in't that –

Amelia   See Sir Somebody is calling on our shepherdess tonight and once Sir Somebody has had her, then I'll have some capital. And I'll be looking to invest.

Tull   No. Tally shop –

Amelia   And I reckon dress up my old stock. Launch 'em afresh. Take these two girls. Rigged well –

Cranton   Oh yes, Mother. New markets for us.

Amelia   Rigged well they could fetch a fair price.

Bolton   Thass right.

Amy   That'll take work. Make these two fresh?

Cranton   Oh no. We was beautiful once. Wun't we, Mary?

Bolton   Thass right.

Amelia   So just you ask him where you can find –

Tull   No. That in't the manner of thing I had in mind.

Bolton   See, told you. Giving up the shop.

Martin   No. You in't gonna do that, are you?

Tull   I dunno. I wanna ask him –

Martin   But we gotta carry on, we gotta do that, there's new stock –

Tull   I gotta decide. Now leave us be. All of you. Just widow and husband and past and future to decide. Please.

They all start to exit.

Amelia (*to* **Amy**)   Come. Let's get you ready for Sir Somebody.

Amy (*to* **Cranton** *and* **Bolton**)   You must be in the next room and when I make a noise so – (*stamps on the floor*) – you must make a noise so: baaaa!

Bolton   Oh Lord. Who'd be a whore?

Exit **Amelia**, **Amy**, **Cranton**, **Bolton** *and the remaining mourners. Pause.*

Martin   You heard her. New stock and we'll –

Tull   Thass enough from you, boy. Leave a widow in peace.

Martin   Mrs Tull –

Tull   Peace.

Exit **Martin**. *Pause.*

Tull   Stephen. Speak to me.

Pause. Enter **Princess**. **Tull** *doesn't see him.*

Stephen, love. Wanna tell you, wanna ask you, Stephen.

Princess   Waste of time. Dead's dead ask me.

Tull   Oh no.

Princess   See when Mother died –

Tull   Dun't want to know about you! Dun't want to know about Mother!

Princess   Thass right. Anger. That's how it took me.

Tull   Is that right?

Princess   Vicious all me life I was. And then when Mother died – Lord, didn't know no bounds. Fighting. This un didn't look at me right, this un didn't speak to me right – smash 'em. Strike out with me fists. That how you feel?

Tull   Yes.

Princess   But then I think: Mother's dead. And I think: life goes on. And I think: put on one of her dresses.

Tull   That dun't seem right.

Princess   Thass what I thought. Dun't seem right. And I carried on: anger, fighting. But all the time dress is in a trunk calling me. And I thought: no, can't. Mother'll come back and tell me no.

Tull   Thass right. 'Thass my dress, son, and you got no right.'

Princess   But one day, feeling was too strong. And I went to the trunk and I put on that dress.

Tull   'No, son, no.'

Princess   And oh putting on that dress I felt such . . . peace and such calm.

Tull   'Don't you go swishing about, son. Gave birth to a man and a man's what I wants you to be.'

Princess   No. Never spoke to me. Cos she's dead and I'm alive and I worn her dress from that day to this.

Tull   We still got things to discuss. He'll tell me . . .

Princess   Now he's gone –

Tull   No.

Princess   I'd be good for the shop. See, I'm a character. Everyone loves a character. Everyone calls out to me: Howdeedo, Princess, and I call out: Howdeedo. And with a character –

Tull   Shop might close.

Princess   No, you gotta –

Tull   I need to ask him. Please.

Princess   Any time you want me, you just call out: Howdeedoo, and I'll come running.

Tull   I'll remember.

Exit **Princess**.

Stephen. Listen love. I been thinking and I . . . Oh, Stephen. I in't up to tallying. Little mouse, Stephen. In the dark with a needle, thass me. Little mind, little voice. Dry old, barren old body. I can't . . . Come back, love. Just a few minutes. 'Thass alright, my love. You sell the shop and move on.' Stephen. Please.

Enter **Martin**. *He carries a large bundle.*

Martin   Look! Look! Look!

Tull   What you got there, Martin?

Martin   New stock. Look.

He opens the bundle and pulls out some very grand dresses.

In't that wonderful? See? In't that something'll fetch a good price? And here. Now – you ever seen fairer than that?

Tull   Where it all come from?

Martin   Business'll take a turn with this, wun't it? Once word is out, we got this in stock, there'll be customers crowding in morning and night.

Tull   Where you get it?

Martin   It's what he would want. Business got to go on.

Tull   They stolen goods?

Martin   Dun't matter.

Tull   Thought so. Martin. Thass wrong. Stolen goods.

Martin   But that's business.

Tull   Not this business.

Martin *sighs*.

Tull   Or you'll swing, boy. That what you want?

Martin *shrugs*.

Tull   Well, I'll make sure you do. Because I'll go to the constables myself, see?

Martin   No you / bloody well won't.

Tull   I shall. I love a hanging. I'll follow that cart through the streets and every rattle of the wheels I'll be calling: 'I told you so, I told you so.' Last thing you see as your neck goes crack will be me with a 'Didn't I say so?' on my lips. And there won't be no ballads or stories about you. Boy who stole dresses. Nobody'll remember that.

Martin   You reckon? Then you do without me, see? You get by on / your own.

Tull   Oh, I shall / I shall. I'll do that.

Martin   You see how long you keep / going without me.

Tull   You go back on the streets. You live like an animal. Go on. GO ON.

Pause.

Well, there's a fair old row, in't there?

Martin   You got a big old mouth on you.

Tull   Big as yours. Don't want to see you hang. Want you to take care of yourself, see? Because . . .

Martin   Because . . . ?

Pause.

You gonna write it in the book? Thass what Master always did.

Tull   I don't know how.

Martin   You'll work it out. Here.

Martin *gives* **Tull** *the ledger.*

Tull   Can't work it out.

Martin   Mrs Tull, you gotta . . . I'm looking to you. I in't Man, I'm Boy. Boy needs protecting, guiding, boy needs . . . Look after me. Thass your duty.

Tull   Love, I in't up to that. I'm frightened.

Martin   You wanna little beer, calm yourself?

Tull   Well, maybe I should.

Martin *goes to pour* **Tull** *a beer.*

Martin   None left. They must have been awful drinkers.

Tull   Right enough. More drinking than mourning I should say.

Martin   I could run and fetch you some beer.

Tull   Yes. A little more beer and then to bed. Here.

She gives **Martin** *a coin from her purse.*

Just mind you come straight back. You're an awful wanderer.

Martin   Don't mean to be.

Tull   I'd say to him: Oh, that boy's an awful wanderer. One day he'll wander off the edge of the world and they'll be no one there to catch him. Where do you go, Martin, when you're a-wandering?

Martin   Nowhere.

Tull   Take a lot of time going nowhere.

Martin   Nowhere special.

Tull   Well – jug of beer and then straight back. Thass straight back.

Martin   Voice big as that, you could run a tally shop.

Tull   You reckon?

Martin   Oh yeah. You can be Master now.

Tull (*laughs*)   Don't know about that.

Exit **Martin**. **Tull** *goes over to the stolen dresses. Picks one up.*

Well, in't that . . . Very fine. (*Another dress.*) Ooo, this'd fetch a good price. (*Another dress.*) Needs work but . . .

Looks at ledger.

Well and maybe I could . . .

Searches through ledger.

Goods in, goods in. Goods in!

Writes down first item.

Well and that in't a bad hand. Come on then, girl. Write 'em.

Scene Three

'Motto 3'

Chorus
>Apprentice boys go to the bad
>So watch 'em night and day
>And mark the scene that now unfolds:
>*The 'Prentice Led Astray*

Moorfields at night. Men silently cruise up and down. **Martin**
crosses with his jug of beer.

'Eros' song'

Eros
>Let Phoebus blaze it through the day
>His wagon burning bright
>For once diurnal course is run
>Comes Eros and the night.
>
>Arise you swain – no slumbering
>Oh heed the call of the night
>My arrow's sharp, my bow is stretched
>Here's Eros, here's delight.
>
>Arise! Arise!
>Up up and rise!
>And risen follow me
>And risen follow me
>And risen follow me.
>
>Let Eros guide you through the streets
>To ev'ry man a mate
>Oh fly my arrow from the bow
>Your passage true and straight.
>
>The prick of Eros' arrow's sweet
>It enters swiftly in
>And once sweet prick is known to man
>His pleasure can begin.

Oh come! Oh come!
Up up and come!
And coming think of me
And coming think of me
And coming think of me.

The tally shop. **Tull** *is working on the ledger by candlelight. Enter*
Martin.

Martin   Know it was a long time. But Cook's was out of
beer. So I went up James's and they was out of beer and –

Tull   All these years, Martin. All these years, working in
this shop.

Martin   Then I went up Swinfield's and Stratten's but –

Tull   All these years and here was me never saw the
beauty of figures.

Martin   I wun't wandering. Know it looks like – well, I
weren't.

Tull   Come. See. Look at that. Just you look at that (*ledger*).
Thass beauty, in't it? See that – down the page. Swelling,
accumulating up . . . 'til . . . there. Total. Then carried
forward . . .

Martin   What's that? That in't Master's hand.

Tull   Oh, you're sharp, boy. In't you the sharpest? Well, if
it in't Master's hand must be . . . Come on. Come on. Work
it.

Martin   Is it . . . ?

Tull   Thass my hand. Thass all my hand. Thass my ledger
now. And this is my shop.

Martin   You decided?

Tull   I decided. We're carrying on, boy. On we go.

Martin   Oh yes! Yes!

He grabs **Tull** *and dances her around the shop. They both whoop. Then suddenly,* **Tull** *stops.*

You crying?

Tull   Crying? No. Just . . . tired. All them figures. Big responsibility I got now, innit? Bed for me.

Martin   What about the beer?

Tull   Take a cup up with me. Now – just mind you dun't go out a-wandering.

Martin   Oh no. In't gonna wander ever again. And thass a promise. Do a bit of work, I reckon.

Tull   Thass a good boy. You gonna miss Master?

Martin   Yes. . . . Thass a lie. No. In't gonna miss Master. You?

Tull   Course. Always.

Exit **Tull**. **Martin** *sits and sews. Enter* **Orme**.

Orme   This is a pretty place. It's all colours and shapes here, isn't it? I like that.

Martin   What do you want? You be on your way.

Orme   Which way?

Martin   Out the door.

Orme   But then what? That's the trouble with me. Don't know which way to turn. I turn this way, then I think: no that way. Turn that way, then I think: no, should turn the other way. Do you understand?

Martin   No.

Orme   That's a great shame. Felt sure you would. Saw you up Moorfields.

Martin   Oh yeah?

Orme   Just now. Walking up Moorfields. And down Moorfields. And up. And . . . Why's that then?

Martin   On an errand.

Orme   See you up Moorfields a few times.

Martin   Might have done.

Orme   You hear what they call Moorfields?

Martin   No.

Orme   Sodomites Walk. You never heard that?

Martin   Never.

Orme   Oh yeah, you take a piss up Moorfields. Take a piss against a wall and all of a sudden there's one man to the left of you and two to the right of you and they're all taking a piss too. And then one man'll reach out and play with the other one's prick. And t'other man'll reach out and touch your prick. Don't you think that's frightening?

Martin   What do you do?

Orme   What's that?

Martin   Man touching your prick. What do you do?

Tull (*off*)   Martin. Martin.

Orme   You ever have your prick touched?

Martin   No.

Orme   Well, you feel such shame and then you feel lost and you don't know which way to turn.

Orme *hides behind the workbench as* **Tull** *enters.*

Tull   Martin. Martin. Everything alright in here?

Martin   Oh yes.

Tull   Thought I heard – You muttering to yourself?

Martin   Might be.

Tull Well, don't. Enough tongues in the world without you sitting there wagging on the job. Shush while I sleep.

Exit **Tull**. **Orme** *emerges*.

Orme That your mother?

Martin No.

Orme You act like she's your mother.

Martin No I don't.

Orme And she should like to be your mother.

Martin I've got work to do.

Orme Please talk to me. I'm still scared. Can't get it out of my head. Those men touching each other. And that man reaching out to me. Ugly with his lust.

Martin I don't want to know about that.

Orme Please.

Martin I don't want to know about you.

Orme Please. Don't say that.

Martin I want to get on with my work. Not right. Men wandering in the dark. Thass all wrong.

Orme Lost souls, in't they?

Martin Yeah. Burning up in Hell on Earth.

Orme But what they to do? No home. Mother and Father wun't have 'em. So – out into the night and . . . grope away. Give 'em a home and that'd all be different. Let your molly be a family. Let your molly be Father or Mother.

Martin Oh no. That in't possible.

Orme And let 'em live in a molly house. Thass what I say.

Martin That in't gonna happen.

Orme   Oh no?

Enter **Kedger**. *As he does,* **Orme** *hides.*

Kedger   You seen a lad?

Martin   What sort of lad?

Kedger   Small lad. Fair face.

Martin   What is it? Thief?

Kedger   Oh no. Not a thief.

Martin   Murderer?

Kedger   No. Apprentice. I upholster and he's my lad.

Martin   Run off, has he?

Kedger   No. Not run off. But he wanders. And then he gets lost. And then he gets into awful trouble.

Martin   What sort of trouble?

Kedger   You seen him?

Enter **Philips**.

Philips   The boy in here?

Tull (*off*)   Martin. I told you. No wagging.

Enter **Tull**.

Tull   Oh. Shop's closed. Come back tomorrow.

Martin   They're looking for a lad.

Tull   Well, wrong place for that.

Martin   Apprentice boy who's lost.

Tull   Where you see him last?

Kedger   Moorfields.

Tull   Long way from Moorfields here. Why you come searching in my shop?

Philips   Saw him come down this way.

Tull   Well, only lad here's mine. In't that right, Martin?

Martin   That's right.

Tull   So you best be on your way. Can't distract the lad when there's work to be –

Tull *has been moving to the bench and now she discovers* **Orme**.

You. Out of there.

Orme *emerges*.

Tull   This the one?

Kedger   Thomas!

Orme   You gonna beat me?

Philips   No.

Orme   Oh please. I've earned it.

Philips   We've been worried to distraction.

Orme (*to* **Philips**)   Oh, Mother, forgive me.

Tull (*laughs*)   What's that you say, boy? (*To* **Philips**.) Called you Mother.

Kedger   This one of your games, boy?

Tull   You in't no mother.

Philips   No. But wun't do no harm if he wants to call me mum, will it?

Orme   Oh yes. Mother. (**Philips**) And Father. (**Kedger**) Because my real father was a beater of children and animals. And my mother was transported long ago for her wickedness. So now we must play at families. I'll be child.

Kedger   And I'll be Father.

Philips   And I'm . . . I'll play at Mother, for the boy's sake.

Tull Don't think the Lord intended . . .

Orme Lord intended each of us to have a father and a mother and if Nature don't provide 'em, we must do what we can.

Tull Well, it dun't sound right to me.

Philips Come. Back to bed.

Orme Can we go up Bartholomew Fair tomorrow?

Philips He wants to see the Rabbit Woman.

Kedger With the rabbits coming out of her cunt? That's all a trick if you ask me.

Philips Hush. Let the boy have his illusions. Grow up and he'll lose them soon enough.

Kedger Alright then, Bartholomew Fair it is.

Orme Oh, thank you. Thank you. (*To* **Martin**.) Will you come with us?

Tull Oh no. He can't. Work tomorrow.

Orme Room for one more, isn't there?

Tull No time for pleasure. His head's filled with trade. In't that right, Martin?

Kedger Then we'll bid you good night.

Tull Good night.

Exit **Kedger**, **Orme** *and* **Philips**. **Martin** *goes back to his sewing.*

Tull That's it. Work to be done. Man was put on this Earth to work. And if he don't he becomes awful effeminate.

Martin Is that right?

Tull Oh yes. Man who don't labour, man who don't produce, man who lies back and watches the world goes by, man like that gets awful womanish. Then no woman wants

him and every man despises him and he sees out his days
alone and despised. So just you mind that.

Martin (*mutters*)   Yes, Mother.

Tull   What's that?

Martin   Said: Yes, Mother.

Tull   Well, good. Me and you and Business now, boy, and
thass all the world to us. So here's what we're gonna do.
Work night and day. Dress up the old stock, in with the
new. And then in with the customers. And you're gonna fit
'em and I'm gonna drive the bargains – and ooo I'm gonna
drive 'em hard.

Scene Four

'Motto 4: New Stock'

Chorus
New stock brings Tull new customers
A penny earned brings more
But still there's danger up ahead
A Bargain With A Whore.

The tally shop. **Tull** *is helping* **Bolton** *into a dress.* **Amelia** *is
watching.*

Tull   Thass it. Very fine.

Amelia   What a pleasure this is, my dear. See you back in
business.

Tull   New stock's always a pleasure, innit? No pleasure
finer I should say.

Amelia   The months passed and they all said: Tull's is
closed and the widow wun't open again. But I said: No, just
working up the stock. And here you are: open for business
once more . Of course there's some as say you haven't got
the head for it.

Tull   Oh are there now?

Amelia   But I tell 'em – no. Mind that one. Looks like a little pinched thing couldn't make boo. But that's deception. Punch yer teeth out to protect her shop, I say.

Tull   Well, in't you got the measure of it?

Enter **Cranton***, in a dress.*

Cranton (*to* **Bolton**)   How do I look?

Bolton   Well enough.

Cranton   Feels good. It's a good cloth. Come. Run your hand over it. Here.

She takes **Bolton***'s hand and runs it down the dress.*

See. Feels good, dunnit? Clean and fresh. And now I feel clean and fresh.

Bolton   Soon be spoiled. There's always mud and men to spoil a dress.

Cranton   But for now . . .

Bolton   You're a dreamer, girl. Dreaming's foolish in a whore.

Amelia   So. Come, Mrs Tull. Name your price. How much a dress a day?

Tull   Sixpence.

Amelia   Sixpence? Thass more than before.

Tull   Better stock than before.

Amelia   But sixpence . . .

Tull   What? Do you ask me for charity?

Amelia   No. Not charity. But favourable terms.

Tull   What terms?

Amelia   Threepence a dress a day.

Tull   Threepence? Threepence? Oh no. I in't doing that.

Amelia   Then we must look elsewhere. Come, girls, dresses off. Up Crawl's.

Tull   Well, maybe you better do that.

*Enter **Amy**, from rear of shop. She is struggling to get into a dress – an elaborate affair with a nautical theme. **Martin** follows her. **Amy** looks at herself in the mirror.*

Amy   Oh, but in't I fine? Knew London would suit me. Oooo – I'm riding the waves. Carrying my goods into port.

Tossed sir, tossed sir, tossed by the sea
Looking for a harbour – O lend a hand to me.

Tull   Oh yes. That's very fine. See, in't that good? Threepence a day? Oh no. You wanna pay a good price for that. Thass worth an investment. Martin – lace her up.

Amy   Stick me on front of a ship, I reckon. Sailors in the rigging, eyes on me. Wun't that be fine?

Tull   Thass the idea. Wants this dress, dun't you?

Amy   Oh yes.

Martin *is pulling at the laces on **Amy**'s dress.*

Martin   In't gonna go.

Amy   Pull harder.

Cranton   Oh, Amy. Is your belly grown? Mary, Amy's belly's grown.

Amelia   What's that?

Amy   Must be London.

Bolton   Must be men.

Amy   What you mean?

Bolton   When's the last time you bled, girl?

Amy   I don't . . . weeks . . . months maybe.

Cranton   And you in't wondered?

Amy   Thought . . . London. Good life. Thought maybe now I was earning Lord's saying: See, girl, you in't cursed no more.

Amelia   Well, that's spoiled goods now, innit? Fresh in with a bloom, I thought, but no – belly on her already. Thass your price halved, girl. Stupid, stupid child.

Tull   That's a blessing, baby.

Amelia   No. That's a curse.

Tull   Don't know what you're talking about.

Amelia   Baby? That'll suck the youth and the beauty and the life out of her, baby will.

Amy   Please. Don't want to be Mother.

Tull   You think that now.

Amy   No. No. Don't want it inside me.

Tull   You see. Mother's instincts'll come and then –

Amy   Mother's instincts? Don't want Mother's instincts. I in't a fucking animal.

Bolton   Baaaaa.

Amy   Bitch. Bitch.

Amy *lashes out at* **Bolton** *but* **Amelia** *holds her back.*

Amelia   Thass enough. I'm Mother here.

Bolton   Baaaa.

Amelia   And I say enough.

Cranton   Mother could sort you, couldn't you, Mother?

Amy   How you mean?

Cranton   Mother's got the art, in't you, Mother? See, when Mary's belly blew up –

Tull No.

Cranton Mother, will you fix her?

Amelia If she pays the price I might.

Bolton Pain's awful bad.

Amy How much?

Tull No. Don't you let them thoughts into your head. That's killing and killing's sin and sin's damned and damned's torment for ever. That what you want? No, you don't.

Amy But I in't ready.

Tull See, baby comes then Nature speaks to you.

Amy No. Can't hear nothing.

Tull Then listen harder. Cos there's women as spend their whole lives praying and praying for infants to come. Praying right to the day when their body dries up and Nature passes 'em by and there in't no hope left. So just you mind that. (*To* **Amelia**.) Dun't kill the infant.

Amelia But business tells me kill it.

Tull And I say don't.

Amelia Can't afford to. Unless . . .

Tull Yes?

Amelia You could hire the dresses cheap. Keep down our costs. Then I could –

Tull No. I can't.

Amelia Then she can't hold on to the child.

Tull Maybe I can . . . fourpence.

Amelia Cheap? That in't cheap.

Tull Three.

Amelia   No. Penny a dress a day.

Tull   Penny? I can't . . . penny.

Amelia   Penny or else we can't afford . . .

Tull   Penny and she'll keep the child?

Amelia   May God smite me hard if she don't.

Tull   Alright . . . a penny a dress a day.

Amy   But I don't want an infant.

Amelia   Good for business, girl, you're having it.

Amy   Oh no. No.

Amelia   Say thank you, girls.

Cranton/Bolton   Thank you, Mrs Tull.

Exit **Amelia**, **Amy**, **Cranton** *and* **Bolton**.

Tull   Well, better write in the book. Ledger, Martin.

Martin *fetches the ledger*. **Tull** *writes*.

Tull   Not the Big I Am now, am I? Oh, Martin. Numbers dancing again. What we gonna do? I can't bargain with a whore. Whores is hard.

Martin   New customers.

Tull   But who?

Martin   New stock there's gotta be . . .

Tull   Who but a whore's gonna hire to dress up as shepherdess or nymph in glory or Queen of Spain?

Martin   Gotta be someone.

Tull   Then we better find 'em, boy. And quick. Before we starve.

Scene Five

'Motto 5: Dame Fortune'

Chorus

Dame Fortune spins her wheel around
And lives are lost or made
Just when she thinks that all is lost
The Widow Finds New Trade.

The tally shop. **Orme** *at the counter. Enter* **Martin**.

Orme   Good day to you.

Martin   What you doing here?

Orme   Shop's awful quiet. Thought: he's bound to be working. Great bundles of thread and cloth. But you're idle, in't you? So come play, Master Idle.

Martin   I in't playing. There's no games here.

Orme   Come. Say I'm an old whore with a face of patches and a cunt of death. And you gotta rig me up cos the King's sent for me so he can take his pleasure.

Martin   She don't want you here. She says you're womanish. Says you're a snare. So you go back where you belong. Back into the dark. Up Moorfields. And wandering and groping and –

Orme   No. Cos – to speak true – Moorfields means nothing to me now. And thass your doing.

Martin   How so?

Orme   Now all I think about is you. And I try to get you out of me head. And I'm up Moorfields and it's: Whoever the fuck wants to fuck me, fuck me. And it's: The stranger the stranger I'm fucking the better. But then in the act and I close my eyes and still I see your face.

Martin   Yeah?

Orme   Yeah. So I had to come to you and tell you and win you. What do you say? Speak true to me. What's in your heart?

Martin   I don't know.

Orme   Heart's speaking. Listen to it. Listen. What's it saying?

Tull (*off*)   Martin.

Martin   Out. Out.

Orme   Oh no, I in't going out. But – round the back. Thass something I could do. You deal with her and I shall be waiting for you. Round the back way.

Orme *hides. Enter* **Tull**.

Tull   That customer?

Martin   No.

Tull   Well, you call if customer comes.

She turns to go. Bell rings. Enter **Amelia**, **Bolton** *and* **Cranton**.

Oh Lord. Whores in't welcome here no more.

Amelia   Dresses returned.

Martin   Three out. Two back. Thass wrong.

Amelia   Thass new girl. She's run off.

Tull   What's that?

Amelia   New girl. We in't seen her. She's run off.

Tull   In my dress?

Amelia   Well, it seems that – yes. Run off in the dress.

Tull   Then I'm gonna find her, see? I'm gonna find her and I'll get my dress.

Amelia   But what about these girls?

Tull   Fuck 'em. Bitches. Martin – you mind the shop.

Tull *starts to exit, followed by* **Amelia**, **Cranton** *and* **Bolton**.

Amelia   Can't let one girl's / selfishness spoil it for the rest.

Tull   You hire from the / tallywoman you return when due.

Bolton   But, Mother –/ what about us?

Cranton   Something popish for me, Mother.

Exit **Tull**, **Amelia**, **Cranton** *and* **Bolton**.

Martin   Thomas. Thomas.

Martin *searches for* **Orme**. **Orme** *emerges in a dress*. **Martin** *doesn't see him at first but then:*

Martin   Take that off.

Orme   There's a butcher. Comes a-wooing me tonight.

Martin   You best put that back.

Orme   Butcher comes. 'Oh, wash your hands. For aren't they covered in blood and won't they spoil my dress?'

Martin   Give it me.

Orme   And butcher says: 'I can scrub all I like but still there's blood on me. For haven't I spent a life in slaughtering of cows and pigs and chicks? There ain't nothing can ever wash away all that blood.'

Martin   Thomas.

Orme   'Oh, but red on your palms and red under your nails, it turns Kitty's stomach so.' 'Well, that's how it is with me and you must take me how I am.'

Martin   Off!

Martin *grabs* **Orme** *and tries to get the dress off him*.

Orme   Take care, Butcher, take care. For although I'm only a poor, sweet girl, I can put up a fight.

They fall to the floor.

Oh, Butcher, mind my lace. Mind my hair. Mind my face.

Martin   Not so strong now, eh, miss?

They lie still for a moment. They get the giggles.

Do you paint?

Orme   No.

Martin   But your skin is so fair.

Orme   As ever Nature made it.

Martin   And your brows are so fine.

Orme   As ever Nature gave me.

Martin   And your lips are the reddest as ever I saw.

Orme   Nature too.

Martin   No. No. I'm sure you paint.

Orme   I tell you I don't. Come. Taste 'em and see.

Martin *kisses* **Orme**.

Martin   You're right. No taste of paint at all.

Orme   Now – your turn. Now you shall be Kitty and I shall be Butcher.

Orme *starts to take off the dress.*

Martin   But – I wanna be Butcher.

Orme   But you can't be Butcher all the time. Sometimes you must be Kitty.

Martin   Why?

Orme   Because I want you to.

He holds out the dress. **Martin** *hesitates.*

You in't scared?

Martin No. Just . . .

Orme Then come.

He helps **Martin** *into the dress.*

The butcher's been waiting all day long. Smiling at the customers. And chopping at a leg and at a breast and stringing up a ham, do you know what the butcher's been a-thinking of? Do you?

Martin No.

Orme The butcher's been waiting for night to fall when his Kitty comes to him and work is over and pleasure begins. There.

Martin *is now in the dress.*

Orme How do you feel?

Martin . . . Foolish.

Orme Don't look foolish.

He leads **Martin** *to a mirror.*

Orme See. As pretty a miss as ever walked the world.

He kisses **Martin**'s *neck.*

Orme Now – you ready for the butcher?

Martin No. I want . . . I want a different game.

Orme Yes?

Martin Sisters together. You be Kitty and I shall be . . .

Orme Hannah.

Martin Hannah? Ugh. Never cared for Hannah. Susan. You be Kitty and I'll be Susan.

Laughing, **Orme** *starts to put on another dress.*

Martin Now Susan – Susan is a lazy slut. For isn't her father a merchant and aren't all the riches of the Indies hers and doesn't she spend all her days lying back with a: Will it be the pineapple or the pomegranate today? With what shall I fill myself? Susan can't be stirred 'til one day there's a knock at her door.

Orme *knocks*.

Martin   And it's Kitty Fisher.

Orme   Her neighbour.

Martin   Her maid.

Orme   Neighbour.

Martin   Maid. Kitty, now I look at you, you're a very pretty thing.

Orme   Thank you, miss.

Martin   Do you like pomegranate, Kitty?

Orme   Ain't never had none, miss.

Martin   Then come taste, Kitty, come taste.

Martin *and* **Orme** *kiss. Enter* **Kedger** *and* **Philips**.

Kedger   Well, here's a to-do. Come looking for a lad and find two little misses. World of surprises, in't it, Mother?

Philips   More wonders in the world than we dreamed of, Father.

Kedger   Come, boy, home.

Orme   Two big brutes in our chamber. Oh, Miss, what are we to do?

Kedger   Thass enough, boy. Dress off and off home.

Philips   Oh, Father. Let him have his sport. For now I look at 'em they're very pretty girls.

Orme   Oh beware, sister, beware. For when men praise, in't they after your maidenhead?

Martin   Thomas.

Kedger   There's upholstering a-waiting, Mother.

Orme   Oh, sister, let us live out our days as virgins and as we go through Heaven's gates we'll lift up our skirts and say: See, our maidenheads are here. And they'll have kept a special place for us with all the virgins.

Martin   Don't wanna play this. He made me.

Kedger   Thass the way with the lad. Always a game too far. Come. Home.

Orme   I in't doing it. I in't.

Philips   Come now, Father's anger is up, Thomas.

Orme   No Thomas here. Just Kitty and Susan here. Kitty and Susan in love and no need for Mother nor Father. Oh, Susan, Susan.

Martin   No. Don't want you.

Orme   Don't hurt me, Susan.

Martin   Game's over now. Susan's dead and gone and Martin's back. So just you be on your way. Just playing, see?

Orme   Oh yes?

*He grabs **Martin** and pulls him up to the mirror.*

Tell everything in a face. Just you take a look. That's a molly face. And that body. You listen to it. Those hips screaming: molly, molly, molly.

Martin   Off me. Off me. Off.

Martin *pushes* **Orme** *away. Pause.*

Philips (*to* **Orme**)   Come, chuck. Can't force a body when the body in't willing.

*He takes **Orme** in his arms and kisses him.*

Kiss from Mother.

Kedger   An' a kiss from Father.

Kedger *kisses* **Orme**.

Philips   That better now?

Orme   Thought he wanted me.

Philips   I know, love. But now you've learned. Thass the world and if you wander in it it'll drown you in its lies and trickery.

Martin   Thomas – didn't wanna – I just . . .

Kedger   Come. Thass it. Kiss the lad and make amends.

Martin *kisses* **Orme**.

Orme   And now we're family, in't we? Kitty Fisher. Susan Guzzle.

Martin (*laughs*)   Guzzle?

Orme   Guzzle.

Kedger   It's ever a new game with him.

Orme   And Mother's . . . Miss Selina.

Philips   Thass a good un.

Orme   And Father's . . . Hardware Nan.

Kedger   Oh Lord. In't you the strangest child?

Orme   Kitty Fisher. Susan Guzzle. Miss Selina. Hardware Nan.

He runs around, throwing dresses in the air.

Come dress and play, dress and play. / Miss Selina – for you. Hardware Nan. What you gonna wear? Oh, dress and play. Dress and play.

Martin   Thomas. Take care there. / Thomas. Mind the stock. Thass – Thomas!

Kedger   Thass enough now, boy. / Thass too much.

Philips   Father – let him have his fun.

Orme *gives a dress to* **Kedger** *and a dress to* **Philips**.

Orme   Thass for you. / Thass for you. Come dress and play. Let's all play families. And we're living in the molly house.

Martin   No. Can't use the stock like that. Thomas.

Tull (*off*)   You hire from the tallywoman, you return when you're due, see?

Martin   Oh Lord. Can't be found. Out the back.

Orme   Stand and face her.

Martin   No. Out the back. Please. Please.

Martin, **Orme**, **Kedger** *and* **Philips** *hide behind the screen as* **Tull** *enters with* **Amy**. *They are pursued by the* **Princess**.

Tull   See, miss. I won't be messed with. You return when due.

Princess   No. Leave her be. Don't –

Tull   Now off with that. And there's extra too for late return. You understand?

Pause.

You listening to me, miss? See, I in't mouse you thought I was. I makes the rules and you follow 'em. Now dress off and pay up cos I ain't hiring to you or your sisters no more.

Pause.

Must I take it from you? Well, if that's the way, I shall.

Princess   Thass a man's anger, that is.

Tull   No business of yours. This is me and customer.

Princess   Found her wandering. She in't right. (*To* **Amy**.) Something's happened to you, in't it, my love?

Tull   Turned thief. Thass what's happened.

She moves towards **Amy** *– smells her breath.*

Oh. Drunk are you? Well, seems to me, you can pay for the drink you can pay for the dress. Here, miss, here.

Princess   No. In't just drunk. There's something . . .

Tull *and* **Princess** *begin to remove* **Amy**'s *dress.*

Tull   What's this spoiling the cloth?

Tull *pulls away the dress to reveal the underskirt. It is drenched in blood.*

Amy   Blood wun't stop. Told me: pain, blood at first. But then it's over. But now won't stop. Just wanted it out of me. Make it stop.

Pause.

Tull   Dress off.

Princess   Mrs Tull –

Tull   Dress off.

Amy   Didn't want to be Mother.

Tull   So kill it? Reach up into your belly and rip it dead? Well, miss, it's pain eternal for you. That's Nature's cursing you, that's Lord cursing you and – yes –that's me cursing you too.

Amy   No. Dun't put that on me. Please.

Princess (*to* **Amy**)   Come, come. There's no curses here.

Tull   Oh, in't there? What I wun't have give to have my belly blow up like that –

Princess   Lost child didn't know what she did.

Tull   Well, dress is ruined now. Thass the stock spoiled.

Princess   Wash her up. Let her rest.

Tull   Dress off her and on her way.

Princess   Wash her, rest her. Thass what my heart says.
And thass what I'm gonna do. (*To* **Amy**.) Thass it. You
come with me.

Princess *starts to lead* **Amy** *to the rear of the shop.*

Tull (*to* **Princess**)   Where you going in my shop?

Princess   You say you wanted to be Mother. Can't be
Mother when it's all stock and ledgers.

Tull   Thass . . . Mother looks after her own.

Princess   Mother dun't look on pain and confusion.
Mother in't body and babies. Mother's in your acts.

Tull   Easy for you. Playing at Mother. But me. I'm in the
real world. And thass hard. So – can't forgive. Can't forget.
Gotta look to my stock.

Princess   There in't nothing of Mother in you. And
maybe there never was.

Exit **Princess** *and* **Amy**.

Tull   Stephen? Stephen? You there?

Silence.

That world better than this one, Stephen?
Well, I bloody well hope so. Cos I want something better
than this. And I bloody earned it. Stephen? Well, if that's
the way of it, then I wanna little pleasure down here. Bloody
great handfuls of Joy on Earth. Thass what I want.

Silence.

Stephen. Know you're bloody listening. Know you're
bloody watching. So why don't you fucking well show
yourself? STEPHEN! STEPHEN TULL, JUST YOU
COME OUT HERE AND LISTEN TO ME!

Enter **Martin**.

Tull   Martin. Whatever are you wearing?

Pause. **Martin** *steps forward.*

Martin   Ain't Martin. It's Susan. Susan Guzzle. Mistress Susan Guzzle.

Tull   Oh, is it now?

Martin   And Susan's awful cross with her mother for being such a sad bitch when Susan needs her mother so.

Tull   And why does Susan need her mother?

Martin   Body's changing, Mother. Titties starting to grow. There's hair between my legs. And there's blood coming out of me. And I needs Mother to show me what to do.

Enter **Orme**.

Orme   And me too, Mother.

Tull   What's that?

Orme   Oh, Mother, don't you know your Kitty Fisher? The poorhouse and how they took me away from you? All me life I've been a searching and a searching and now I've found you. Oh, Mum, Mum.

He hugs **Tull**.

Tull   Martin – this is queer sport.

Martin   Ain't no Martin no more, Mum. Hanged hisself from a beam after breakfast. Says to me: Susan, tell the mistress I love her, but I can't stand this world no more. And I says: 'I shall', as the rope tightened round his neck.

Enter **Kedger** *and* **Philips**.

Philips   Oh, Mother, thought we'd lost you.

Tull   Oh, did you now?

Kedger   Oh, the world's an awful cruel place for tearing a family apart, in't it? But it's over now. Family's here.

Tull   Family?

The men all hold **Tull**.

Orme   Oooo – Ma. Thass good.

Tull   Lord. How many children I got?

Kedger   Oh, hundreds, Mother.

Tull   Well, ain't I been busy?

She pulls away.

Tull   What am I – ? Can't be playing these games. Come on, Martin. Thass enough games.

Martin   No. Playing's best thing we got. You wanna be Mother? Then – play.

Orme   Yes, Ma. Come play.

Tull   But . . .

Philips   All these years, Ma, with just your picture in my locket for company. Shipped off, cutting 'bacca in the sun 'til I thought me skin was gonna burn away. And stealing and saving and stealing and saving so I could pay the fare home, home to Mother.

Tull   No. In't playing. But . . .

Orme   Yeah?

Tull   Maybe . . . hiring. Thass something I could do. You wanna dress?

Philips   Oooo yes, ma.

Tull   And you?

Kedger   Yes, Ma.

Tull   Then let's get the measure of you.

Tull *starts to measure them. Enter* **Princess**.

Princess   What's this?

Tull   These are my customers, Princess. They're after hiring of dresses.

Princess   But . . . they're too big. They'll pull at the seams.

Tull   Then I'll have to stitch in extra.

Princess   But, Mrs Tull, men in dresses –

Tull   Said the kettle to the pot.

Princess   But that's different. I'm a character.

Tull   Oh no. Hundreds of 'em, in't that right?

Kedger   That's right.

Tull   And I shall hire to 'em. A shilling a dress a day. That's my price. Take it or leave it. Come on, Princess. You wanna work? Then lend a hand. See, I'm moving out of whores. Whores are finished and I'm moving into mollies.

Princess   But, Mrs Tull – these men are sodomites.

Tull   You're sure?

Princess   Every last one of them.

Tull   And what of it?

Princess   It in't right.

Tull   In't right? And who are you to judge?

Princess   It turns my stomach.

Tull   For that is the beauty of business. It judges no one. Let your churchman send your wretch to Hell, let your judge send him to Tyburn or the colonies. A businesswoman will never judge – if your money is good.

Princess   But sodomites –

Tull   And if your sodomite is a good customer, then that is where I shall do my business.

Princess   It in't natural.

Tull   Oh yes. I shall turn my head away when prick goes into arse. And I shall look to my purse. And all will be well. You wanna work? You want employment? Then come. I'm calling on you. Howdeedo, Princess, howdeedo. Now rig 'em.

Orme   Ma. Can we have a house?

Tull   For all the mollies?

Orme   For all the mollies.

Tull   Oh yes. Thass it. Molly house. Come, Princess. Rig and pay. Rig and pay. Molly house is open for business.

Princess   Mrs Tull –

Tull   Oh no. In't Tull no more. Tull's dead and buried see. From this day on all shall call me Mother.

More **Mollies** *appear.*

'End of Act One'

Mollies
Rejoice!
A home at last
Mother is here now
Sorrow is past
Sorrow's past past past!

Rejoice!
We'll live in light
Our bodies are ours now
Hearts are our own now
Our choice
Our promised land.
Rejoice! Rejoice!

God *and* **Eros** *appear.*

All
Reconciled, reconciled!
God and Eros reconciled!

Pleasure in profit
Profit in pleasure
God and Eros reconciled!

God

Morality is history
Now profit reigns supreme

Eros

And love can speak its name out loud
Now business loves a queen

All

We are the future
We are the light
This is our time
This our right

This is our Happy End
But this is just the start
This is a marriage
Of purse and arse and heart

God bless us one and all tonight
Let us live in Heaven's light
We're sure that what we do is right
So shit on all those who call this sodomy
Shit on those who call this sodomy
Shit on those who call this sodomy
We call it fabulous.

Act Two

Scene Six

2001. A loft apartment. **Josh**, **Charlie** *and* **Tina**. **Tina**'s face is covered in piercings.

Charlie   Do you know what I call her?

Josh   No. No, I don't.

Charlie   Tell him.

Tina   No.

Charlie   Go on. Tell him what I call you.

Tina   The Iron Lady.

Charlie   It's fucking incredible. Another day, another piercing. Every time I come home she's done another one. Fucking blood everywhere. And I goes to her – for fuck's sake clean yourself up. Cos I in't doing it again. In't that right?

Tina   Yeah, that's right.

Josh   Absolutely. Have you got the – ?

Charlie   She's got fucking hundreds of 'em. I don't understand it. Why d'you do that to yourself?

Tina   I dunno.

Charlie   I mean, I give her anything she wants. But – oh no. Daytime telly, piercings. Thass her life.

Josh   Well, whatever turns you on.

Charlie   Yesterday I come home, she's got the mirror on the floor and she's stood over it – starkers – blood –drip, drip, drip – and she's doing her . . . whassis . . . her . . .

Tina   Labia.

Charlie   Thass it. Doing her labia.

Josh   Really?

Charlie   I had a right go at her. But she won't stop. I think she's disturbed.

Tina   No. Just –

Charlie   Yes you are. Total fucking headcase.

Tina   Don't you talk to me like that, you fucking –

Josh   Actually, I've got a few. Piercings.

Charlie   Yeah?

Josh   Yuh. Tits. Knob. Just not the face, you know. Work. Have you got the coke?

Charlie   I want to have kids.

Tina   Don't.

Charlie   Be great, couple of kids.

Tina   Says you.

Charlie   Thass why I deal, right? Put a bit by so we can bring 'em up. Move to the country, I reckon.

Tina   I don't like the country.

Josh   I could really do with a line.

Charlie   But I mean, how the fuck is she gonna have a kid? Poor fucker would have to fight through half a ton of ironwork just to get out of her.

Tina   Oh, fuck off.

Charlie   And she couldn't feed it. There's more metal than nipple.

Tina   Why do you always do that? / Why do you always put me down like that?

Charlie   I'm just saying, I'm just telling him, that's all, babe.

Tina   Well, don't. / Cos I don't want to hear it, alright?

Charlie   Just having a laugh. If you can't take a joke.

Tina   Oh, fuck off. Fuck off.

Josh   Hey. Hey. Hey. Listen. Listen. Have you got the coke?

Charlie   Special delivery.

He produces a large bag of coke.

Quality.

Enter Will, carrying a video cassette.

Will   Oh hi. Dropping off supplies? Fabulous. I thought we had enough for a week and then these silly queens came over for supper and – hoover, hoover – you would have thought Colombia was about to fall into the fucking ocean.

Charlie   Having a bit of a party, are yer?

Josh   Something like that.

Will   More of an orgy really.

Charlie   Right.

Will   Well, a sex party.

Josh   A sex-party-orgy-underwear sort of thing.

Tina   Uuugh.

Josh   Sorry?

Tina   I said: Uuuugh.

Charlie   Don't worry about her. She's just a bit – Whass the word?

Tina   Homophobic.

Charlie   She dun't like poofs. But I tell her: poofs, they got it sorted.

Will   Is that right?

Will puts the video into the machine.

Charlie Not like before, is it? Now it's your poofs know how to enjoy themselves, it's your poofs with the money nowadays. Poofs running the country now, in't there? Do all my business with the poofs. Well, you don't get the hassle, do you? (*To* **Tina**.) Poofs paying for your piercings, that is.

Will presses play. A porn video plays.

Tina Uuuugggh.

Charlie Fucking hell. He's going for it with that fist, in't he?

Josh Oh, I met that one once.

Charlie What the one with his –?

Josh Yes. At a party in Chicago. I would have slept with him only I had a flight the next morning and he had to get up early for church.

Doorbell rings. Exit **Josh**.

Charlie I wanted to try all that stuff. Gang-bang stuff. Took her up this fetish club, didn't I?

Tina Yeah.

Charlie Told her: I'm not getting pissed or nothing but . . . She didn't like it. Said it was –

Tina Boring.

Charlie That's the trouble with her, see.

Will Ennui.

Charlie No. She gets bored easily.

Enter **Josh** *and* **Tom**.

Josh You're very early.

Tom   I know, sorry. It's just I don't know the area so I left a lot of time. But actually it's really easy to find, isn't it? If you want me to go away and come back –

Josh   No, no.

Tom   This is really nice. Like in a magazine, isn't it?

Josh   That depends what magazines you read.

Tom   Yeah, right, right. (*Sees* **Tina**.) Oh. Is there gonna be women? Only I –

Charlie   No, mate, you're alright. We're pissing off.

Josh   I'll get your money.

Exit **Josh**.

Tom (*to* **Tina**)   Sorry. Was that rude? I didn't mean to be rude. I really like your . . . your . . . (*piercings*).

Tina   Fuck off.

Tom   Yeah, right. Right. Sorry. I'm probably talking too much. I just did a couple of E. I always feel better. New people, new situations an E. Because naturally I'm sort of introverted but with an E . . .

Charlie   It's legs in the air and off you go, you dirty slag.

Tom   Yeah, right. I'm wild. Up for it at compuserve dot com. That's my address. Which gets me quite a lot of attention actually. Oooo – is that charlie?

Will   Would you like some?

Tom   Can I? Ooo, I'm mad for the charlie, me.

He opens the bag and rubs the coke on his gums.

Oh, that's good. Bit of charlie's good after a couple of E, isn't it? Cos sometimes with the E . . . Well, I find it hard to connect with people so I take the E and I connect with them and I go to bed with them and I can't always perform. You know. Which is the downside of E. I mean, not always.

Well, not all that often actually. Often I go like a train. That's what they say. Loads of blokes say that to me. Just sometimes . . . Did you know you're bleeding?

Tina   Wassat?

Tom   You've got blood down your leg.

Tina   Oh. Right.

Charlie   Fucking hell, I told you. Pierced her . . . wassis . . .

Tina   Labia.

Charlie   And now it wun't stop. Clean yourself up. Where's your bathroom?

Will   Here. Let me show you.

Tina   Come and help us.

Charlie   Fucking headcase.

Exit **Will**, **Tina** *and* **Charlie**. **Tom** *takes more coke. Produces a bottle of water. Does another E. Doorbell rings.*

Tom   Excuse me. Excuse me. Your –

Doorbell rings. Exit **Tom**. *Re-enters followed by* **Edward** *and* **Phil**. **Phil** *carries a large bag.*

Edward   Hi. Edward. Phil. Sorry, we're so early. But the roads were clear and – Gosh. Quite a place you've got here.

Tom   Oh, it's not actually my –

Edward   Brought along some toys. Hope you don't mind. Phil.

Phil *hands* **Tom** *the bag.* **Tom** *unzips the bag.*

Edward   Quite a collection we've got, haven't we, Phil?

Tom *pulls an enormous dildo out of the bag.*

Edward   Dildos, butt plugs, et cetera. Always like to give them an airing, don't we, Phil?

Phil   Yeah.

Edward   We go to quite a lot of these things. We're old hands so to speak. Always worth travelling for a good bit of action. Isn't that right, Phil?

Phil   Oh yeah.

Edward produces a video camera.

Edward   No objection to the camera, I hope?

Tom   Oh no, no.

Edward   There's always a shy one of course but I have to say most people find it an enormous turn-on, don't they, Phil?

Phil   Yeah.

Edward   Hoping to add a little watersports to the collection this evening actually. Do you . . . ?

Tom   No.

Edward   Pity. Right then.

He produces a very complicated harness from the bag.

Now then. How's about I slip into something a little less comfortable?

Tom   Oh yeah.

Edward   Through here? Super.

Exit **Edward** *with harness.*

Phil   Sorry about him. He dominates, doesn't he?

Tom   That's alright.

Phil   Watch out if you fuck him. Back-seat driver. Up a bit, down a bit. Faster. Slower. I have to gag him.

Tom   Yeah?

Phil   He's grateful for it really.

Enter **Edward**, *half-undressed.*

Edward   Phil. I'm gonna need a hand.

Phil   In a minute.

Exit **Edward**.

You been to one of these before?

Tom   Well, sort of . . . well, no. No I haven't. Exciting,
isn't it?

Phil   Is it?

Tom   I think so. Really, really exciting. Because actually,
you know, I only came out recently. You know, when I
moved to London. Two months and I've like totally
changed. Like: there's Old Me and New Me.

Phil   Is that right?

Tom   Oh yeah. And Old Me was like . . . stop me if I'm
talking shit, alright? Sometimes on the E, I . . .

Phil   Alright.

Tom   Well, I know this is mad but I feel like Old Me was
living in the Olden Days. History and that. Really, really
old-fashioned. All scared and no sex and no drugs. And now
there's New Me – and I'm like totally Today. I'm Now. Do
you know what I mean?

Phil   Oh yeah.

Tom   Time machine. Two months and I've travelled
hundreds of years into the future. Only the future's like now.
I mean, look at me. Clubs. E. Shagging all sorts of blokes.
It's great. And now this.

Enter **Edward**, *wrestling with the harness.*

Edward   Phil.

Phil   Coming.

Exit **Edward**.

Tom   My first actual live-sex party. Fucking great, isn't it?

Phil   Yeah. Great.

Enter **Charlie**, **Tina**, **Josh** *and* **Will**. **Tina** *is bleeding badly.* **Charlie** *has a towel covered in blood.*

Tina   Get your fucking hands off me. / I don't want to be touched.

Charlie   Just trying to clean you up, thass all.

Tina   I can't stand you touching me. / I hate that.

Josh   Hey, hey, come on, come on. / Let's just cool it.

Will   Watch where you're going. Blood on the – hey. Not the sofa.

Charlie   Come on, babes. Let's clean you up.

Tina   I'm alright. I'm alright.

Tina *goes to sit on the sofa.*

Will   Not the sofa. Not on the sofa.

Tina   Just leave me alone.

Tina *is just about to bleed on the sofa.* **Will** *pulls her away from the sofa.*

Will   No!

Tina   Get your hands off me. You fucking poof! I hate you. I hate you all. I hate your money. I hate your big houses. And I hate your fucking sofas. Fucking sticking your fists up each other. Fucking disgusting. / Fucking sick.

Will   Alright, that's enough. / Because actually now, I'm getting really offended.

Tina   Oh, is it? Oh, is it really? Come on then, let's have yer.

Tina *puts up her fists and goes to fight* **Will**. *Suddenly, she faints.* **Charlie** *catches her.*

Charlie   Lie her down.

Josh *picks up* **Tina***'s legs.* **Charlie** *starts to move them towards the sofa.*

Will   No. No. Not the sofa. Through here.

Will *leads the way as* **Josh** *and* **Charlie** *carry* **Tina** *off to the bedroom. As they do,* **Edward** *enters. He is now almost into the harness and is wearing a leather-studdded jockstrap with motorcycle boots.*

Edward   Phil, I really need you to –

Phil   Yeah, yeah.

Exit **Phil** *and* **Edward***.*

Tina   What happened?

Charlie   It's alright, babe. Everything's going to be alright.

Exit **Will** *and* **Charlie** *and* **Josh***, carrying* **Tina***.* **Tom** *stands lost. Enter* **Eros***.*

'Phoebus Reprise'

Eros
  Feel Eros chasing through your veins
  Through heart and head and skin
  This feeling's all, this chemistry
  So let the game begin.

Tom   Wow. You're beautiful.

Eros
  Let Eros still the hand of time
  May youth be ever yours
  With age comes grief but youth is free
  So play and leave remorse.

Eros *takes* **Tom***'s hand, sings him a song. As he does so,* **Will** *and* **Josh***'s flat melts away and becomes the molly house.* **Mollies** *swarm around* **Tom** *and* **Eros***.*

Tom   This is really, really exciting.

Eros
   Come play, come play
   Up up and play
   And playing dream of me
   And playing dream, playing dream
   And playing dream of me.

Scene Seven

The molly house. Four **Mollies** *– whooping and goosing each other. Enter* **Princess**.

Princess   No no no. (*To one* **Molly**.) See, you must take extra care with this 'un. This is for gliding. You can't go rushing about in this one. You must – like this.

He glides. The **Mollies** *giggle.*

(*To another* **Molly**.)   And you, miss. Got my eye on you. Prancing about after paramours, lifting them skirts. That in't right. Dressed up fine and fine you must be.

Mollies *giggle.*

Princess   Oooo, but you mollies is silly creatures. If it weren't for her I wouldn't stick this.

Mollies *giggle.*

Princess   In't one of you understands how to carry a dress. If all you want's a jig and a fuck then why rig up as woman, eh?

Enter **Tull**.

Tull   Here she is. Here's Mother.

Mollies *rush to* **Tull**, *kiss her hands.*

Tull   Thass it. Welcome. Well and in't the Princess rigged you fine? Gonna be a good night tonight. Best night ever at Mother's.

Mollies *cheer.*

Tull   Now, my dears, beer waiting for you through there. Some of your sisters already here. And more to come. Dancing'll start soon. So go on – off you skip.

Exit **Mollies**.

Princess   How did you find him?

Tull   Very low, Princess. Lower un low.

Princess   Thass what I thought.

Tull   'Oh, Mother,' says he. 'In't I been foolish. Thought Kitty Fisher loved me.'

Princess   Can't trust your molly. Didn't I say?

Tull   And I says: 'Susan, love, I'm sure he does love you. Just it comes out peculiar.'

Princess   I should say it does. Fucking any man or boy that comes in here.

Tull   Oh no. It in't bad as that.

Princess   Bad as that an more. Last night alone saw him a-petting and a-bundling with three of 'em severally and then – jug of beer later – three of 'em together. Can't get badder than that.

Tull   Thass youth.

Princess   Thass wickedness. Thass the sodomite way. Fuck 'em once and then find another.

Tull   But I'm sure in my heart Kitty loves his Susan Guzzle still.

Princess   That sort dun't know love.

Tull   Them too – true love.

Princess   And how can you tell?

Tull   Mother's instincts. You seen Kitty?

Princess   Mrs Tull –

Tull   What's that? Still harping on Tull? Ain't heard that in a while.

Princess   Well and maybe you should. See, these games –

Tull   No. Don't pull me back to Tull, love. Mother now and I in't never been happier. Now, see, I got a plan. Win Kitty back for Susan. You watch. Tonight's the night for Mother's plan. And once tonight is done – Kitty and Susan's gonna be reconciled. Got Susan ready now all I gotta do's find Kitty and –

Princess   You know what they call you, your mollies?

Tull   What's that?

Princess   Clap.

Tull   Thass just one of their names.

Princess   Mother Clap.

Tull   And where's the harm in that? If it makes 'em happy then Mother Clap I shall be. You seen Kitty?

Enter **Kedger**, **Philips** *and* **Lawrence**. *They are all in men's clothes.*

Tull   Well – what have we here?

Kedger   Customer for you Mother.

Tull   Well, in't you a fine un? In't he a fine un?

Philips   Found him up Moorfields.

Tull   Oh, nothing up Moorfields nowadays. Well, nothing but the poxed and prickless. So come and welcome to Mother's.

Lawrence   Right. Howdo.

Tull   Thass a shilling in.

Lawrence   Right.

Lawrence *gives her a shilling.*

Tull (*calls*)   Ned! Customer! And a shilling for the dress.

Lawrence   The dress?

Tull   Thass right. Princess and Ned'll dress you.

Lawrence   But I don't –

Tull   Oh, all wear dresses here. In't that right?

Philips   Thass right.

Lawrence   But I in't the type.

Enter **Amy** *dressed as a man, carrying a dress.*

Lawrence   What's that?

Tull   Thass Ned.

Lawrence   That a lad?

Tull   Lad now in't you, my love?

Amy   Thass right.

Tull   Didn't have much of a time of it as Woman, did you, Ned?

Amy   Thass right.

Tull   Did awful wicked deed as Woman. Sent infant, wun't you? New life growing inside Woman here. And she ripped it out and bled and bled. But I found it in my heart to forgive. And since Ned chopped at his hair and slipped into his breeches he's been a great help. Although his temper's awful fierce – so mind him. Now. What's your molly name, my dear?

Lawrence   How do you mean?

Tull   All have names at Mother's. China Mary, Primrose Mary, Garter Mary, Orange Mary, Pomegranate Moll. Young Fish Hannah, Old Fish Hannah, Miss Selina, Kitty Fisher, Kitty Cambric. Flying Horse Moll, Thumbs and Elbows Jenny, Hardware Nan –

Lawrence   Susan.

Tull   Oh no. For we already have our own Susan Guzzle. So let's . . .

Philips   The Mistress Girl of Midriff.

Tull   Oh yes, lovely.

Enter **Orme** *in a dress, watches.*

Tull   Right, Princess, Ned, off with the Mistress Girl and rig her.

Philips   And us too, Mother.

Tull   Course. And you too. Rig 'em all.

Exit **Philips**, **Kedger**, **Princess**, **Lawrence** *and* **Amy**.

Orme   Well and in't he a fine un? I shall be offering a curtsey and a 'Will you dance?' to that one tonight.

Tull   What? And no thought of your Susan?

Orme   Course. Always a thought for Susan.

Tull   Susan'll be thinking of you. Loves you bad.

Orme   And I love Susan.

Tull   You sure of that?

Orme   And I shall come back to Susan. Just – we must fuck who we will. Else what's the point of a molly house? Might as well be Man and Wife like rest of the world. 'Go on, Susan,' I say. 'Have another. Have a score. I'll love you all the more.' But silly girl just moons it about and waits and waits. Thass Patient Griselda not my Susan Guzzle.

Tull   You was happy enough to play the marrying game.

Orme   And that was lovely, Ma, and you married us good but then . . . Oh, Ma, I get bored so easy. Do you think that's bad? Am I a bad un?

Tull   No, love. In't none of Mother's children bad. I in't here to judge. Just got to find a way so you're happy and Susan's happy.

Orme   But how?

Tull   Ah, well . . .

Orme   Ask me, happiness is like Fortune's wheel. One's up, t'other's down.

Tull   No. I got a plan. New game. Bring you and Susan together. You wanna play?

Orme   What game's that?

Tull   You shall see. You must wear this so (*gives* **Orme** *a blindfold*) and wait in the next room and we will fetch you when all is ready. Will you play along?

Orme   Is it a good game, Ma?

Tull   It's a marvel.

Orme   Then I shall.

Exit **Orme**.

Tull   Susan! Susan!

Enter **Martin** *in a dress.*

Tull   Susan. You better get yourself ready.

Martin   There in't no point, Ma.

Tull   Well, thass where you're wrong.

Martin   I lost him, Ma, and that's that, gotta face facts.

Tull   You dun't want to give up that easy, girl. You love him?

Martin   I hurt all the time. Is that love?

Tull   Thass a part of it. Gonna win him back you see. You trust your ma?

Martin   Course.

Tull   Then do as Mother says cos new game's about to begin.

Enter **Lawrence**, **Kedger** *and* **Philips**, *now dressed as mollies, and* **Princess**.

Philips   Well, in't she a pretty miss?

Tull   Oh yes, Mistress Girl. Thass lovely.

Lawrence   I feel foolish.

Tull   Well, you looks a picture.

Sound of **Mollies** *within.*

Ooo, dancing's about to begin.

Exit **Martin**. **Mollies** *enter, including several musicians. The* **Mollies** *dance.*

'Mother Clap's Maggot'

Mollies
Whoever the fuck wants to fuck me, fuck me
Cos you are the finest, the finest I've fucked.
Whoever is lying beside me, sighing
Whoever is coming inside me, dying
The stranger the stranger I'm fucking the better
But closing my eyes and I still see your face
So we'll fuck til the day when we're finally fucked
Til we lie in the sod, til we rot
And we'll smile at the worms as they gnaw at our flesh
And tell them how finely we fucked.

Tull   The words you use – enough to make a body burn with shame. (*To* **Orme**.) Now you – blindfold on and into the next room.

Exit **Orme**.

Welcome, welcome one and all to Mother Clap's Molly
House.

Princess   No, you don't wanna –

Tull   Knows what they call me, Princess. An I like it.
Mother Clap. Thass me.

Tonight rules is left at the door. What do you wanna be
today? Maid or man? You decide. Husband or wife? You
choose. Ravished or ravisher. Thass for you to say. Cos
there in't no bugger here gonna tell you what to be.

And if you wanna take your paramour in private, take
'em to a room, lock the door and find your pleasure there,
then Ma says: Good. And here's the key.

She holds up a key.

And I don't charge much. But I am a woman of business.
And if anyone says I in't paying I says – I says it sweetly and
I says it with love – but I says: Bugger off.

Now tonight. Tonight's a special night. Cos now we got a
game like one that in't ever been. Cos tonight our Susan
Guzzle – well, let's call Susan Guzzle forth. Music there.

'Birthing Scene'

Musicians play as **Tull** *recites.*

Susan, Susan, in't the time to hideaway
Susan, Susan, Mother dear
Says: Show yourself and say
'How doo' to all your sisters gathered here.

Enter **Martin**. *He has a pregnant stomach.*

Tull   Oh, Susan – what's this? A belly chuck?

Martin   Thass right, Ma. Up and up it blew.

Tull
Oh, Susan, in't this wond'rous luck?
Oh, Susan, Mother's proud of you.

Martin

    An' shall I have to wait for month on month
    Before an infant peeps from out me cunt?

Tull

    Oh no, my love. Ma's art shall do its work on you
    Right here and now is when the infant's due.
    But labour's hard – you know the pain is great.

Martin   Oh, pain, Ma, don't know if –

Tull

                    But wait!
    Let's bring the father forth. He'll see you through.
    The love of one who's good and true
    Means we can bear life's pain and suffering.
    The father there and let the birth begin.

More music – fuller and louder. Two **Mollies** *exit. Re-enter with* **Orme** *blindfolded.*

Tull   Kitty Fisher – are you listening?

Orme (*laughs*)   Yes, Ma.

Tull

    Kitty – glad tidings of great joy I bring to Earth.
    You ever heard of how a virgin once gave birth?

Orme   Yes, Ma.

Tull

    Well, tonight there's something queerer yet
    Unmask him there and let
    Our Kitty wonder at the sight.

Orme's *blindfold is removed.*

Orme   Susan!

Tull

    Come womb – the time is right
    Let waters break, our Susan's due
    Come precious child

Ma waits, world waits, love waits for you.

The molly musicians play a beautiful slow piece as **Martin***'s labour progresses. Finally, silence as the baby – a wooden doll – is pulled out from* **Martin***'s skirts.* **Tull** *lifts the baby up to the Heavens – then slaps the baby's bot***tom**.

Mollies   Waaagh.

Tull *hands the baby to* **Martin**.

Orme   Susan. What is this?

Martin   Infant love. Mine and yours. Come see.

Orme   But I dun't want infant.

Martin   Look, that's your eyes. My nose. Our mouth. Come, love.

Orme   Thass a stupid game. You told me –

Tull   Oh yes. Thass a very pretty child. Thass lovely, Susan. Come on, Kitty.

Orme   I in't playing that. That's stupid. Seems to me you better let me choose the games now on. Who wants a dance there? Come. Let's dance.

Tull   Just you hold baby in your arms.

Orme   Oh no. Didn't want molly house so it could all be marrying and babies. (*To* **Martin**.) Sorry, love. But there in't no pleasure in that. (*To* **Lawrence**.) Will you dance with me, sir?

Lawrence   I in't much of a dancer.

Orme   I shall show you the way. There in't much to a jig. Soon have you jigging. Come, sisters. Away and dance.

Exit all but **Tull**, **Martin** *and* **Princess**. *We can hear the* **Mollies**, *off, dancing and singing during the following.*

Martin   You ruined it all now, in't you?

Tull   Susan, love –

Martin   Lost him now.

Tull   No.

Martin   Don't think I don't see it, cos I do. Baby? Thass not what I want. Baby – thass you. Thass you're wanting. Can't make me into what you want to be. Cos that goes nowhere. I don't want this. Want him. And he's gone for ever.

Exit **Martin**, *leaving baby.*

Tull   Oh, Princess. What am I to do?

Princess   Mrs Tull. I'm a man. Man's feelings. And I wanna tell yer –

Tull   What's that?

Princess   What a man likes is to be around a woman. A woman of life and vigour. A woman worth watching. Mrs Tull, I've been watching you.

Tull   Oh, have you now?

Princess   Do you think that's bad – man watching you?

Tull   Oh no. I like that. But you're . . .

Princess   A man. A man's feelings. Oh, let me show you.

Tull   I got money to count.

Princess   Husband's dead. You gotta kiss the living.

Tull   No. I don't want to do that.

She moves to exit, turns.

What would I be kissing? Man, woman or hermaphrodite?

Princess   Close your eyes.

Tull   Yes?

Princess   Close your eyes and see what pictures come into your head. Alright?

Tull   Alright.

Princess *kisses her.*

Princess   What do you see now?

Tull   Man. (*He kisses her neck.*). Woman. (*He kisses her breasts.*) Hermaphrodite.

Princess   And which do you want?

Tull   Oh, Princess –

Princess   See, Mrs Tull, I'll be anything for you. Just tell me what you want me to be and that's what I'll make myself. I'm a blank and you can choose. Ain't no dignity in it, is there? I know that. Where's his dignity? you're saying. Well, I say: bugger dignity and bugger pride. Cos what's pride when love comes a-calling? And thass what I got for you, Mrs Tull – love.

Tull   Princess –

Princess   So come – what's it to be? What do you want?

Tull   I want . . . I want . . . I want what my dry old body in't never gonna give me, that's what I want. I want life inside me – here. You gonna give me that? No, you in't. Ain't nothing gonna make this live. In't no game gonna make that good.

Princess   I in't playing a game.

Tull   Oh, it's all games here. Mother Clap? Thass a game. Princess? Game? We're all playing, in't we? Best we'll ever have. So, come my mollies. Mollies – come.

Enter men in their underwear, including **Phil** *and* **Josh**.

Tull (*to* **Phil**)   You wanna take your paramour? Then come take him, take him.

Princess   Mrs Tull –

Tull   The sodomites are here, Princess. Sodomy's arrived.
You wanna look aside? Turns you stomach still, dun't it?
But it's pleasure to them and that's enough for me.

Princess   I can't stay for this. I'm going now. Packing up
and going see? Tell me stay, Mrs Tull. Love you. Love you.
Alright. Last you'll see of me. Thass goodbye for ever now.

Exit **Princess**. **Phil** *starts to fuck* **Josh**.

Tull   That's it. Go on. That's it. Pleasure 'til morning
comes. Pleasure 'til Judgement day. Oh yes. Pleasure,
pleasure, pleasure. Pleasure ever more.

Scene Eight

*2001. Loft apartment. The party is in full swing. Music playing.
Various men wander through in their underwear.* **Phil** *is fucking*
Josh *over the sofa.* **Josh** *sniffs from a bottle of poppers. There is a
porn video playing.*

'Pleasure'

Eros
   Pleasure pleasure pleasure's here.
   You wanna touch me? I gotta think about that.
   You wanna take me? OK.
   You wanna have a good time?
   Come on come on come on.

   You got the sweetest booty of any boy in town
   I love that booty booty and I am going down
   And down down down

   Shake it take it don't fake it
   Make it real sister
   Go sister, you're such a ho sister on video sister
   Make me sing Miss Thing
   With your ring a ling a ling a ling

   Tomorrow's never coming

And yesterday is gone
Now is how I wanna be
So bring the pleasure on
And on and on and on

Phil   How you doing?

Josh   Yeah. Great.

More fucking. Enter **Charlie** *from bedroom, carrying the bloody towel. He calls back to* **Tina**.

Charlie   Just – lie still. Keep pressing on it. You're gonna be alright.

He sees **Josh** *and* **Phil**.

Alright?

Exit **Charlie** *to the bathroom.* **Phil** *uses the remote to rewind the video.*

Enter **Edward** *with the camcorder. He videos them.*

Edward   Oh yes. Always like to get the highlights on the camcorder, don't we, Phil?

Phil   Yeah.

More fucking. **Edward** *continues videoing.*

Edward   I've become rather good at this. And now, of course, you can get these fantastic editing packages. Many a merry evening I spend editing my footage of Phil. Off you go, I say to him. Off you go and have your fun. Bit of sleazy slut action for you. Because I've got you right here with me on tape.

Josh   I'm sorry, I –

Josh *pulls away from* **Phil**.

Edward   Whoops. Hope I didn't throw you.

Josh   No. It's not that.

Edward   There's always a shy one.

Josh Oh no. The camera's fine.

Two men cross the stage and exit.

Edward   Hello. I think the action's just about to shift to
the bathroom.

Exit **Edward**. *Enter* **Charlie** *from bathroom. Enter* **Will** *from
kitchen.*

Charlie   You got any more towels?

Will   What?

Charlie   You got any clean towels? (*To* **Phil** *and* **Josh**.)
Sorry about this, lads. (*To* **Will**.) Only she's still bleeding.
Won't stop.

Will   I'll have a look.

Charlie   Cheers.

He gives **Will** *the bloody towel. Exit* **Will**. **Charlie** *stands
awkwardly watching* **Phil** *and* **Josh** *fucking.*

I try and understand her. I really do. Every other bloke she's
been with has knocked her about. All I've ever done is buy
her whatever she wanted but still she . . . The only time
she's happy is after she's done a piercing. Then next day
she's all moody again and she starts planning the next one. I
mean, what's it all about?

Enter **Will** *with towels.*

Will   Here.

Charlie   Thanks, mate.

Exit **Charlie** *to bedroom.*

Will (*to* **Josh**)   Look. I think maybe we should cover the
sofa.

Josh   The sofa's fine.

Will   Just, you know . . . stains.

Josh   I'll be careful.

Will   Well, just make sure you do.

*Enter **Edward** from bathroom.*

Edward   Phil. Quick. There's rimming.

Phil   In a minute.

*Exit **Will** to kitchen.*

Edward   But it might be over / in a minute.

Phil   I'm busy.

Edward   Honestly, I've driven us all the way up here. / I think the least you –

Phil   I drove us up here.

Edward   – can do – I thought you liked rimming.

Phil   Yeah, well.

Edward   Really, sometimes I just don't understand you.

*Exit **Edward**. **Josh** pulls away from **Phil** and sits on the sofa.*

Phil   Sorry about him. He's always like that. But you get used to it.

Josh   Yeah, right.

Phil   I say I'm gonna leave him. But I never do. He's positive.

Josh   Right.

Phil   And, well, you don't like to leave them when they're at death's door, do you?

Josh   He doesn't seem like –

Phil   A few years ago he was like this little old stick man. I had to feed him, clean him up. And then these new medicines come along and now look at him, running around like a fucking kid. I could move on but I'm sort of stuck with him now. It's alright. We have a laugh. Do you wanna have another go?

Josh   No. Thank you.

Phil   Right. Well, I better go and check on him.

Exit **Phil** *to bathroom. Enter* **Will** *from kitchen.*

Will   What? Finished already?

Josh   Just . . . coming up for air.

Will   And how was he?

Josh   Fabulous. Yeah. Fantastic fuck. And you?

Will   Me? Oh, you know.

Josh   Had anyone fabulous yet?

Will   No. Not yet.

Josh   Well, you wanna get in there.

Will   Yeah, right. Listen –

Enter **Tom**.

Tom   Great party. Really, really great.

Josh   Here we go. Just your type.

Will   No. Not really. Listen. I don't want to –

Josh   Good luck. (*Hands* **Tom** *the poppers.*) Here. You might need these.

Tom   Oh, right. Triffic. Right.

Exit **Josh**. *Pause.*

Tom   Hello.

Will   Hello.

Pause.

Tom   I think you're really attractive.

Will   Thank you.

Pause.

Tom   I hope you don't mind me saying that.

Will   Not at all.

Pause.

Tom   Is he your boyfriend? Josh?

Will   God, that's a difficult question.

Tom   Is it? Sorry.

Will   Oh, it's just so fucking complicated.

Tom   Right.

Will   I mean, we don't fuck any more. Haven't fucked in years.

Tom   I see.

Will   Although sometimes we still do threesomes together if we're in the mood.

Tom   Got you.

Will   But not very often. But we live together. Joint mortgage and all that. And I care about him. Whatever you'd call that feeling.

Tom   Love.

Will   That kind of thing. And he's always meeting people. German boys or Portuguese boys – a Japanese once – and he's always going to live in Hamburg or Aporto or a little place outside Hiroshima – because this time it really is love and he's leaving and all of that. But it never happens.

Tom   Right. Right.

Tom *moves to kiss* **Will**.

Will   Listen. I'm sorry. But you're not my type.

Tom   Oh, I see. So – what is your type?

Will   Oh, I don't know. I forgot a long time ago. (*Indicates porn.*) Well, I suppose that's my type. Until you actually meet them. And then they open their mouth and it's a total turn-off. Look, if you want to suck me off.

Tom   Alright then.

Will   Maybe something will happen.

Tom *starts to suck* **Will** *off. Enter* **Edward**,*with the camcorder.*

Edward   Oh yes. I feel like chicken tonight.

Tom *goes to move.*

Will   No. Don't stop. Don't stop!

Several more men come in.

That's it. That's good. Come on, everyone. Come and look. We're having fun in here. Oh yes. We're having a fucking fantastic time here.

Tom *tries to pull away but* **Will** *pushes him down and holds his head hard.*

Will   I told you not to stop. Good boy. Good boy. That's good.

Tom *chokes.*

Will   Take it all. Take all of it. Who else wants to join in? Why not everyone? Yeah, come on. Everyone join in.

Tom   No.

He pushes **Will** *off.*

I was really looking forward to this evening. This is all I ever wanted. All them years stuck at home listening to me dad: Fucking poofs this, fucking queers that. And I thought: You're history, you. Cos I'm a poof, but I in't telling you. Oh no. One day I'm just gonna up and go. Stick a note on the fridge. 'Fuck the family.' Little husband with his little wife and their little kids. That's history. And I'm the future. This is the future. People doing what they want to do. People being who they want to be. So why . . . ? Why do you have to make it wrong?

Exit **Tom**.

Edward   Do you know, I think I might edit that bit out.

Phil   No. Leave it in. Be good for a laugh.

Edward   Think so? Possibly. Right then. I still haven't got any watersports. Who's going to oblige?

Enter **Charlie**.

Charlie   Listen, lads. Sorry, I don't wanna . . . but she's . . . oh fuck. Sorry, lads. But she's not breathing. Can someone . . . ?

Pause.

Lads. We gotta do something.

Scene Nine

Amelia, **Cranton**, **Bolton** *and the other whores pray.*

'The Whores' Prayer'

Whores
  Father, look down on your children now the customers
    have gone.
  Father look down on our brothel empty – how shall we
    carry on?
  Ev'ry man's turned molly and ev'ry maid's alone
  Father – bring them back from Sodom, bring the buggers
    home.

Bolton   Waste of time you ask me.

Amelia   On your knees, miss, mouth as wide as you can and – up to the Heavens.

Whores
> Father fill your brothels 'til they're brimming, show us joy
> once more
> Father don't abandon me, or me, or me – an honest
> simple whore
> Father – world'll soon be empty if ev'ry man's turned
> queer
> Father – man must lie with maid again – oh bring
> the buggers here.

Cranton   Well – and much good may that do us.

Amelia   Oh, he's listening, miss, and any day now he'll
send us a sign.

The molly house. **Tull** *is counting the money. Enter* **Lawrence**.

Lawrence   Scuse me. I dun't want to be a bother. But
they're all doing it. In public.

Tull   Wait, love. Ma's . . . ten, eleven, twelve . . .

Lawrence   I don't think that's right.

Tull   Well, each finds his own pleasure here.

Lawrence   I mean, Moorfields, thass dark. You get the
odd fumbler when you're in the act – but I push 'em away. I
like to take 'em one at a time.

Tull (*writing in book*)   Twenty-three, twenty-four, twenty-
five.

Lawrence   See, there's still right and wrong, in't there?
And I say: I'm man and I take 'em and thass right. And I
don't watch others and others dun't watch me. Cos thass
wrong. But this lot . . . candles a-blazing, great piles of 'em.
I think that's very wrong.

Tull   Thass how they like it. Thirty, thirty-one, thirty-two.

Lawrence   Well, thass not as I like it. Can I have a key?

Tull   Wassat, love?

Lawrence   For a room.

Tull   Well . . .

Lawrence   I have my shilling. See. Thass my last shilling
but I wanna . . . paramour in private, as you said.

Tull   Yes, I said, love, but see . . .

Lawrence   My money's good.

Tull   But see, love, Kitty Fisher – oh, I know Kitty Fisher
gives it strong with a fine un like you and course you wants
to take Kitty – and Lord knows there's plenty of 'em has
had Kitty – but see thing is Kitty –

Lawrence   It in't Kitty.

Tull   No?

Lawrence   No. That in't my type. I know that type – it's
all fine words and fancy games with that type, in't it?

Tull   Oh yes. Kitty plays awful games.

Lawrence   And that in't the type to – oh, I in't never
spoke to woman like this before.

Tull   Oh, I in't woman, love, I'm Mother.

Lawrence   Well, see if I'm gonna – excuse me – fuck 'em,
I don't want words, words, words and games. I want – they
gotta lie back and take it good.

Tull   And Kitty in't never gonna do that.

Lawrence   And Kitty in't never gonna do that. See, all I
wants an honest simple – excuse me – fuck. I'm a pig-man.
Thass low wages. And there's wife and eight infants to feed.
And wife. Well, wife's insides got messed about with all that
carrying and birthing, so wife, wife – excuse me – wife in't
been worth fucking in years. So when I drive my pigs into
market and selling's done, thass what I want. A – excuse
me – fuck. Thass what makes life worth living. Do you
understand?

Tull   Course, my love.

Lawrence   I dun't think woman can ever understand that.

Tull   Your woman muddles it all up, dun't she? Can't just lie back and – 'Take me.' It's all: 'Take me cos you love me.'

Lawrence   Thass right.

Tull   Or: 'Take me cos I want infant.'

Lawrence   Infants. Thass woman for you.

Tull   Well, I'm Mother Clap. And Clap – let's just say I've give up 'love me' and 'give me infant'.

Lawrence   And now what's left is . . .

Tull   What's left is . . .

Lawrence   What's left is 'fuck me'.

Tull   Well, I suppose that's right.

Pause.

Lawrence   Look, I in't really bothered about lads. The only reason I – excuse me – fuck lads is cos woman's needy and whores want paying. But you –

Tull   Yes?

Lawrence   Seems to me you're . . . woman who understands a fuck's a fuck. You're a – excuse me – fucking wonder.

Tull   You don't want me. Old thing. You want young –

Lawrence   I want a hole. I want to work away 'til my pleasure comes. And there'd be pleasure in that for you too seems to me.

Tull   I got work. Forty, forty-one, forty-two.

Lawrence   Come, can't be running about after sodomites all your life. Look to yourself. Look to me. Come to a

private room. I spill easy. Wun't be more than a few
minutes.

Tull   Oh, love. I'd like that. But . . .

Lawrence *kisses her.*

Lawrence   I dun't kiss as a rule.

Tull   Beer and tobacco. In't tasted that in a long time.

Lawrence   I want you – do something special. Make
noise.

Tull   Wassat?

Lawrence   Make noise like –

Enter **Amy**.

Amy   They're calling out for more beer. Only there in't
none.

Lawrence   You – leave us be.

Amy   Shall I fetch more beer?

Tull   Well, I suppose you better. Here.

Tull *gives* **Amy** *money.*

Amy   This one a bother?

Tull   You just run along.

Amy (*to* **Lawrence**)   I tell you, you're a bother, I'll run
you through.

Tull   Thass enough, Ned. Off you run.

Exit **Amy**.

Lawrence   Whole world's gone arsey-versey. Now come,
up to that room.

Tull   No. I in't doing that.

Lawrence Well then – excuse me but – fuck you. I gotta get a hole. I got a lad willing if you in't gonna – give me the key.

Tull You promise it in't Kitty Fisher?

Lawrence Much better than that.

Tull Then here. And may you find what you want.

Lawrence Oh, how I wish it'd been you. Well – lad's just gonna have to take my anger now, inn'e?

Lawrence *kisses* **Tull** *and exits.* **Tull** *goes back to her money.*

Tull Forty . . . oh, where was I? . . . forty . . . oh, come on, girl, where'd'you leave off? Forty, forty, forty. Forty what? One, two, three.

Enter **Orme** *followed by* **Kedger** *and* **Philips**.

Orme Ma? You seen the pig-man?

Tull Kitty love. Ma's counting.

Orme The pig-man been in here?

Tull Well, maybe he has and maybe he hasn't.

Orme You didn't give him the key, did you, Ma?

Tull I gotta concentrate.

Orme Dun't tell me you give him the key.

Philips Come, chuck, don't bother Ma now.

Orme I gotta know: You give him the key?

Tull Kitty – you gotta learn. Sun don't spin round you. Just cos you got fair face dun't mean you're the only one that's ever gonna be took. Dun't mean you're the only one pig-man's got his eye on.

Orme Oh, I know that.

Tull So maybe you learn from this you gotta be truer.

Orme   Has he got the key?

Tull   Yes. He's got the key. Eight, nine, ten.

Orme   Oh, fuck you, fuck you.

Orme *upsets the piles of money.*

Tull   Kitty!

Kedger   Come, love. Come to Ma and Pa.

Kedger *and* **Philips** *hold* **Orme**.

Orme   He's with Susan.

Tull   No.

Orme   Oh yes. 'See, it's me he wants not you,' says Susan. 'And he's gone to fetch the key.'

Tull   Oh Lord.

Orme   Can't bear to think of him taking my Susan.

Kedger   Your Susan?

Orme   My Susan.

Philips   But in't you always said . . .

Orme   Thass what I always said but now – new feeling. What's this I got inside me, Ma?

Tull   Close your eyes. What you see?

Orme   Green. Brightest green ever.

Tull   Then that's jealousy.

Orme   And is that a good feeling?

Tull   Thass lover's feeling.

Orme   Oh, I don't want to be a lover.

Tull   Then go back and dance and find another.

Philips   Come, chuck, away. Sisters waiting.

Orme, **Philips** *and* **Kedger** *go to exit.*

Orme   Oh, but I can't get Susan out my head. What's that pig-man doing to him, Ma?

Tull   Well, I don't know I'm sure. Old woman like me in't gonna know, is she? Come. Back to the dance.

Private room. **Martin** *and* **Lawrence**.

Martin   Locked now. All to ourselves.

Martin *slips the key into his cleavage.*

Lawrence   Lie down.

Martin   You're fast.

Lawrence   Man's always fast. That's his way.

Martin *lies on his back.*

Lawrence   Other way. On your front.

Lawrence *is getting out of his skirts – he still has his breeches on underneath.*

Martin   Oh, but in't we gonna buss a little?

Lawrence   No. Other way.

Martin   But there's always kisses here. See, if you're working down there, I like to feel you in here too.

Lawrence   And if I'm working down there, I don't want to feel nothing up here, see? So turn over.

Martin   One kiss. Just one kiss.

Lawrence   Come here.

They kiss.

Martin   You taste nice.

Lawrence   Thass the beer.

Martin *caresses* **Lawrence***'s groin.*

Martin   Hello Peter, hello. That good?

Lawrence   S'alright.

Martin   Peter's still asleep, in't he? I'll have to wake him. Wake up, Peter. Wake up. No time to be a-bed. Oh yes. Cock is crowing. Toodleoodleooo! How much beer you had?

Lawrence   Fair amount.

Martin   Toooodleooo! Captain Pintle. Stand to attention. Bugle's going. Doodoodedoo! Oh yes, time to invade the lowlands. Forward march.

Lawrence   Here. Let me do it.

He works himself up.

Get on all fours.

Martin *is on the bed on his hands and knees.*

Martin   Do you like that? Is that how you want me?

Lawrence   Yeah. Like an animal. Like a big old sow. Titties hanging down and all them little pigs sucking on you. Make noise.

Martin   How you mean?

Lawrence   Make noise of a sow.

Martin   I in't never heard it.

Lawrence   Everyone's heard pigs.

Martin *attempts a pig noise.*

Lawrence   No. In't you ever been on a farm?

Martin   Never.

Lawrence   Like this. (*He makes a pig noise.*)

Martin *copies* **Lawrence***'s noise.*

Lawrence Thass good. Now. I'm a big old hog and I'm coming up to you.

Lawrence *makes aggressive hog noises.*

Martin Come on then.

Lawrence Since when has sows been talkers? Do as you're told.

With much grunting and squealing from both sides, **Lawrence** *enters* **Martin**.

Martin Thass – hurting.

Lawrence *grunts and squeals louder.*

Martin Slower there. That hurts.

Lawrence There's slaughterman, takes away hogs that are a bother, you know that? Well, he does. One of 'em goes wrong, hold 'em down and clean cut across the throat, see? So. You a good pig or a bad pig?

Martin Good pig.

Lawrence Right then.

He enters **Martin** *again. It is less painful for* **Martin** *this time.*

Lawrence Oh yes. Oh yes. I'm nearly . . . yes.

Tull *and* **Orme** *appear outside the door.*

Tull Susan? Susan love, you in there?

Lawrence Ignore 'em.

Tull Susan. Mother's got Kitty with her.

Martin Then tell her: Susan's having a high old time. Oh yes! Yes! Yes!

Lawrence No. Grunts only. Oh yes. I'm gonna spill, I'm gonna . . .

Tull Susan, Kitty wants to speak to you.

Martin   I ain't speaking to Kitty. Take me, take me.

Lawrence   Thass it. Work me. I'm close.

Orme   Susan love –

Lawrence *grunts vigorously.*

Orme   Susan love. I been a wrong un. I see that now.
Susan? Them others? They was fucks and fucks is fucks but,
Susan, you – Susan, I love you. And love's love. And it's all
hurting and jealousy and wanting and it's bloody awful and
really I dun't want nothing to do with it – but I got it,
Susan. Susan –I got love for you.

Martin   Yeah?

Lawrence   Don't stop.

Orme   Thass true, Susan. Ev'ry blessed word.

Martin *pulls away from* **Lawrence**

Lawrence   Oh – fuck you.

Martin   You swear?

Orme   I swear. Open the door.

Lawrence   Come back. I'm so close.

Tull   Susan love –

Lawrence   You can't leave off now. Can't just work a
body up and leave him. Come, Mistress Sow.

Martin *turns the key in the lock.*

Lawrence   Oh no, no, no.

Tull *and* **Orme** *come into the room.*

Lawrence   Fuck it. Fuck it. Fuck it.

Orme   Oh, Susan love.

Martin   Oh, Kitty love.

Orme *and* **Martin** *kiss passionately.*

Lawrence   What about me? I'm only asking for a fuck. Is that too much to ask?

Martin   I didn't want to . . . just . . .

Orme   I know, love. Come away. Oh, Susan.

*Exit **Martin** and **Orme**.*

Lawrence   Look, I'm very close. I'm a breath away. Could you just . . . ?

Tull   No, love.

Lawrence   Oh well.

He turns away and masturbates until he comes.

Excuse me. Sorry. I hope I in't been a bother.

Tull   No, love, you in't.

Lawrence   Just when I get the ache . . . there's vulgarity and that and really with a woman around I shouldn't –

Tull   I understand. Here. Kiss for Ma.

She kisses him.

Lawrence   Oh well, back to the country. Back to my wife. Back to my pigs.

*Exit **Lawrence**. **Tull** is just about to go when: Enter **Princess**. He is in men's clothes.*

Princess   Howdeedo.

Tull   Oh, Princess.

Princess   No. In't Princess no more. Stopped all that now see. Gone back to me real name. William. How do I look to you?

Tull   Like a man.

Princess   Like any other man?

Tull   Yes. Like any other man.

Princess Ordinary. Dull. Drab. Wouldn't you say?

Tull Well, yes. Ordinary, dull, drab.

Princess See, I thought couldn't keep hiding behind them skirts. Didn't want to do that no more. See, Mrs Tull. I think about you. All the time. Every minute. Church bell goes 'Tull', man calling out his wares cries 'Tull', open a door and it's creaking 'Tull'. And I can't just let that lie, can I?

Tull Well, no. Suppose you can't.

Princess So I had to come back to you and I wanted you to see me as I am. See William. And he in't special. But he cares about you.

Tull Well, thass good. William.

Princess Yes, Mrs Tull?

Tull You wanna buss a little?

Princess Yes, Mrs Tull.

They kiss.

Tull See a man when you do that. Buss again.

Kiss again.

Tull See a woman now.

Princess No. Thass all finished now. I'm a man.

Tull Saw a woman though.

Princess Try again.

Kiss.

Tull Yes. Definitely a woman.

Princess Is that bad?

Tull No. Felt good. Kiss me again.

Kiss.

Tull   Hermaphrodite.

Princess   Oh Lord. That wun't suppose to be.

Tull   Well, that's how it is. Man. Woman. Hermaphrodite.

Princess   Which of 'em do you want?

Tull   Well, now . . . Want a man . . .

Princess   Yes?

Tull   Want a woman . . .

Princess   Yes?

Tull   And I want . . . hermaphrodite. Want all of 'em. All of you. Oh, lustful thoughts.

Princess   Is that right?

Tull   Will you come to bed, love?

Princess   Mrs Tull . . . I'm a virgin.

Tull   And I in't much in practice but . . . You frightened?

Princess   A little.

Tull   I'll be gentle, love. Now come – to bed. Howdeedo, Princess.

Princess   Howdeedo.

Scene Ten

2001. **Tina** *sits on the sofa. Enter* **Edward**.

Edward   How you doing?

Tina   Yeah. Alright.

Edward   Thought we were going to lose you.

Tina   No. That's just him.

Edward   Bit of a drama queen?

Tina   No. He makes a fuss. I'm alright.

Enter **Charlie**.

Charlie   You sure you don't want an ambulance take you up the hospital?

Tina   No.

Charlie   If you want I can call –

Tina   No.

Charlie   I called your mum.

Tina   You didn't?

Charlie   You want a taxi take you home?

Tina   I dunno.

Charlie   I'll call a taxi. (*Dials mobile.*) Yeah, hello. Can I have a cab to –

Exit **Charlie**.

Tina   See what I mean? Says to me: Have anything you want, go anywhere you want. He's always buying me things and taking me places. Fly me right round the world if that's what I want. I can't stand it.

Edward   Sounds alright to me.

Tina   It's always you choose, babe, you decide. But I can't choose. I just wanna pierce myself. To pass the time. And it doesn't mean anything. Nothing means anything, does it?

Edward   No. Probably not.

Enter **Tom**.

Tom   Basically, I'm a very positive person. So I'm not going to let this get me down. I'm going to learn from this. Because this was a real experience. And that can't be bad, can it? It's like E, isn't it? Like good E and bad E. And if you never took like a really shit E – like E that is basically just a bit of speed and a load of shit – then you wouldn't like really appreciate a totally fantastic E that gets you off your tits until you look at the world and go 'I love you. I love you, world. You're fucking fantastic, you are.' Which is actually what happens more often than not with E. See, I reckon in a few years' time I'm going to be – no offence – really old. And then there'll be time to be sad and serious and all that – but until then it's like Global Disco Family. Am I talking shit?

Tina   Yes.

Tom   Sorry. Does anyone know a club that's still open?

Enter **Will**.

Tom   Excuse me. Do you know a club that's still open?

Will   No. Sorry. (*To* **Tina**.) Well, you're looking much better. (*To* **Edward**.) Thank Christ somebody knew what to do, eh?

Edward   Mmmmm.

Tina   What did you . . . ?

Will (*indicates* **Edward**)   Gave you the kiss of life.

Tina   What? You . . . ?

Edward   Yes. Old trick I picked up somewhere.

Tina   Right. Right.

Enter **Charlie**.

Charlie   Taxi's on its way, babe.

Enter **Josh** *and* **Phil**.

Josh (*to* **Will**)   Listen, we thought we'd go on to a club. You want to come?

Will   No. I'll clean up the mess. I'll see you tomorrow.

Phil (*to* **Edward**)   You coming?

Edward   I don't think so. Rather a lot of editing to do. Not one of our better efforts but still . . . should be able to salvage something. Yes. Video and a bit of a tug on the old love stick and then bed for me, I reckon. (*To* **Josh**.) He's a fantastic fuck. You'll have a great time.

Tom   Take me with you. I won't be a bother. Just I need to share the taxi only I haven't got enough . . .

Josh   Sure. Why not? See you tomorrow.

Exit **Josh**, **Phil** *and* **Tom**.

Charlie   Sorry about the mess.

Will   These things happen.

Charlie   And when you want some gear . . .

Will   Of course. Always going to need a bit of gear, aren't we? Got to be something, make this bearable.

Charlie   Yeah. Right. Right. Well, then, see ya.

A car horn sounds.

Charlie (*to* **Tina**)   Taxi's here. You alright to walk or do you want me to . . . ?

Tina   Fuck off.

Charlie   Yeah. Right. Right. Fucking headcase.

Exit **Tina** *and* **Charlie**.

Edward   D'you see what happened to the butt plug? Got lost somewhere in the mêlée.

Edward *starts searching.*

Will   Don't you ever . . . ?

Edward   Yes?

Will   Don't you want to say: You're mine. And I want you to myself and I can't stand this fucking around. It's killing me.

Edward   Oh no. No fun in that at all, is there?

Will   No, suppose not. Oh fuck. Look at this sofa.

Edward   Soon get that off. Good scrub's all it needs. Now where's my . . . ? Bathroom?

Exit **Edward**.

Will   Oh, fuck it. Fuck it. Fuck it.

Scene Eleven

'Motto 6'

God
> The pain of love is hard to bear
> The joy of love is strong
> And lovers come and fuck and leave
> But business carries on
> Oh business carries on
> Enterprise shall light your darkness
> Business must go on.

The molly house. A large trunk with its lid open. **Tull** *is packing the trunk with linen, pewter, etc. She sings to herself as she goes.*

Enter **Princess**. *He is wearing his dress. He is carrying a heavily laden bag.*

Tull   Oh yes. Dun't you look fine? Wass it like – back in the rig?

Princess   Feels good. I thought . . . somedays skirts, somedays breeches. What do you think?

Tull   Oh yes. Variety's the spice, innit? Let's say breeches or dress during the week and then Sundays . . . (*Laughs.*)

Princess (*laughs*)   Yes?

Tull   Well, on Sundays, Lord's day . . .

Princess   Yes?

Tull   Hows about we Adam and Eve it on Sundays?

Princess   What . . . ?

Tull   Naked as we were born all the day long.

Princess   Oh yes. Naked as we were born. But what if there should be passers-by?

Tull   Then fuck 'em – for in't that how the Lord made us?

Princess   Still – dun't wanna upset neighbours.

Tull   Then you must rig us up lovely out of leaves. Be leaves a-plenty in the country, I should think. Oooo – Sunday can't come fast enough, says I.

They carry on packing.

Princess   You wanna take the ledger?

Tull   No. Ledger's all part of the effects. She's gonna need ledger, in't she? not me.

Princess   Still, we gotta live . . .

Tull   You telling me how to do business?

Princess   No, love.

Tull   I can do business. Don't you fret yourself on that score. I'm renting the house and the business for a good price, see? Just cos I got love in my heart now dun't mean me head can't do numbers, dun't mean these hands can't count coin. So I drove her hard and now we can stretch to a bit of land. And I shall turn my hand to husbandry and you can take in sewing. How does that do you?

Princess   That does me as fine as Heaven on Earth.

Tull   Well and it don't come better than that.

Enter **Martin**. *He is in men's clothes and he is carrying luggage and the 'baby'.*

Martin   Are you petting?

Tull   No, love, we're working.

Martin   Only I'll leave you be if you're . . .

Tull   No, love. Come on. Soon be time to go.

Princess   You tired, boy?

Tull   That was his Kitty Fisher keeping him up.

Martin   No. That was . . . that was . . .

Tull   Was we being awful noisy?

Martin   Terrible noisy.

Tull   Making up for wasted years, in't we, Princess? The old uns is the worst uns, dun't you think?

Martin   I should say.

Pause. He holds up the 'baby'.

I was wandering. Found . . . What d'you wanna do with this? I was gonna leave it. But then I thought . . . maybe Ma wants to play that game. Of an evening, I can, or Kitty can, or you can . . . take it in turns to give birth if that's what Ma wants. What do you say?

Tull   I say . . . I say . . . trunks is awful full and I say . . . best leave the infant behind. Thass what I say.

Martin   You sure?

Tull   Yes, love, I'm sure. In't time for them games no more, is it? Old woman Tull – that's her wanting, that is. And I dun't want none of that foolish bitch no more. And Mother Clap. She's gone too. Goodbye to her. Dun't need me mollies a-skipping and a-fucking around me no more. Good game while it lasted and it filled me purse fit to bursting. So now we can move on. Away from this world. And on to the new. Whatever we are. Just the four of us. Princess, Kitty, Susan and . . . Lord, who am I?

Princess   Wassat?

Tull If I in't Tull and I in't Clap, who am I?

Martin Mother?

Tull No. Not Mother. New name for me. But what? Well, time will tell.

Enter **Orme** *and* **Amelia**. **Orme** *carries several dresses.*

Amelia Oh no, boy. Just you leave them be.

Orme But that's my dress. / I wanna take my dress.

Amelia Oh no. Not yours to take, see? They're mine.

Orme Ma, you tell her – that's my dress and she in't having it.

Tull Well, Kitty love, that in't strictly –

Orme Oh, ma, can't live without me dress.

Tull Well, see, I've leased it all. Lock, stock and gown. It's all hers now.

Amelia And I hire out at a shilling a day. So . . . Of course if you wanna stay in London and hire 'em then I might consider . . .

Tull Thought you was gonna tally to whores.

Amelia Well, now, Mrs Tull, I've been giving that some thought.

Tull Thass what you told me.

Amelia I know that's what I said. But then . . . well, then the Lord spoke to me.

Tull Oh, did he now?

Amelia Oh yes, Lord spoke. And he said to me: It's a bugger's world. And he said: Your man don't really like your woman. And he said: All your man wants to do is find a hole and work away and he said: Arse will always triumph over cunt.

Tull   Oh no, I don't think that's right.

Amelia   And I was sore afraid. And for three days and three nights I fretted. Because what's it gonna be like? In this bugger's world. Bugger King, bugger merchant, bugger cowman. And every maid lost and alone. And not a child born. And soon world'll be empty, just animals like man had never been.

Tull   No. That in't never gonna happen.

Amelia   But still the Lord called me and I thought molly house is full and whore house is empty and so I decided: don't tally, molly. It's the only way to survive. And that's what I intend to do.

Enter **Cranton** *and* **Bolton**.

Amelia   And these girls will run and fetch for me. Isn't that so, girls?

Cranton/Bolton   Yes, Mother.

Tull   Well, just you be good to them mollies, mind.

Amelia   Course, Mrs Tull. Customers are always treated kindly, aren't they, girls?

Cranton/Bolton   Yes, Mother.

Tull   Oh, I hope so.

Amelia (*to* **Orme**)   So come, boy. Tonight's gonna be a grand old night at Mother's. Take who you will. Will you hire and stay?

Orme   Is it gonna be as good as Clap's?

Amelia   It's gonna be better than Clap's.

Orme   Well, that sounds awful good.

Martin   But, love – what about country? What about cottage?

Orme   Oh, Susan. I dun't know whether I can live out all me days in a cottage. Thass her dream. Thass running away from the world. And I in't ready to do that.

Amelia   Then hire, boy, and fuck away.

Orme   Susan – maybe if I stayed tonight. Just for old times. And then I could come to you tomorrow.

Martin   If that's what you want.

Orme   That's what I want.

Amelia   That's it, boy.

Orme   And maybe from time to time I can come a-mollying and maybe if you wanna come a-mollying too . . .

Martin   Well, we'll have to see about that.

Orme   Yes. We'll have to see about that.

Enter **Kedger**, **Philips** *and several* **Mollies** *– all in men's clothes.*

Kedger   Coach is waiting, Ma. Come to make our goodbyes.

Tull   Goodbye, my chucks. Goodbye.

Goodbyes are made. The **Mollies** *help carry out the trunks and luggage as this is done.*

Tull   Well, in't we had some high old times but Ma's gotta go now.

Enter **Amy**, *still dressed as Ned.*

Bolton   Amy. What you done to yourself, girl?

Amy (*to* **Tull**)   Country in't the place you think it is. Country's hard. Thieving and raping in the country same as here. You're gonna need a man looking over you in the country.

Tull   You wanna come with us, Ned?

Amy You're gonna need me.

Tull Then you come with us, Ned. There's a place for you.

Philips Coach won't wait no more.

Tull Come, loves, away.

Exit **Tull**, **Princess** *and* **Amy**. **Martin** *rushes up to* **Orme**.

Martin You'll come tomorrow?

Orme Susan, you musn't nag.

Martin I'll be waiting for you.

Orme Well, that's good.

Tull (*off*) Susan! Susan!

Martin *exits.* **Mollies** *gather round the door and wave them off. The coach's horn sounds until it becomes distant and fades. The* **Mollies** *turn back to* **Amelia**.

Amelia Well and off she goes. But you musn't feel low. Because we're carrying on. And I'm Mother now. And Mother's purse is hungry. So – come. Fill.

The **Mollies** *don't move.*

Orme Come, sisters.

Amelia They in't coming, boy.

Orme What, sisters, off away? And where are you to go? Back into the dark? Oh no. Can't do that.
   So come. Here we can jig and drink and fuck. And anyone of you as wants Kitty Fisher can have me.
   Sisters. This is the best we got.
   So: pay!

The **Mollies** *fill* **Amelia**'s *purse.*

Amelia That's it. And now dance, you buggers, dance.

Orme Music!

'Amelia's 'Maggot'

The **Mollies** *start to dance.*

Amelia   That's it. Beer there beer.

Cranton *and* **Bolton** *fetch beer. The dancing becomes livelier.*

Orme   Oh yes. Dance. Dance. Dance. And on for ever more.

The dancing becomes more and more frenzied. **Eros** *joins the dancers. The* **Mollies** *start to take their clothes off. The music turns into techno. The molly house becomes a rave club as the light fades to nothing.*

Music

In the Royal National Theatre production of *Mother Clap's Molly House*, the accompaniment for 'End of Act One' and 'Pleasure' was pre-recorded. The remainder of the music was played by a five-piece pit band with orchestrations by Matthew Scott. The full score and band parts, and both pre-recorded accompaniments, are available on hire from the play's agent, Casarotto Ramsay & Associates Ltd, National House, 60–66 Wardour Street, London W1V 4ND.

These songs were written to be performed by actors who sang, rather than specifically for singers, and hence there are fewer strict allocations of vocal parts than is traditional. The majority of the songs were performed by male voices (with obvious exceptions) but productions should feel free to adjust where necessary to accommodate whatever balance of genders they prefer.

Further information on the music can be found on the composer's website: www.matthewscott.net or via the play's agent.

Matthew Scott is one of the foremost theatre composers of his generation, having composed music for more than fifty productions, including premières by Harold Pinter, Nicholas Wright, John Mortimer, Jeremy Sams, Mark Ravenhill, Brian Friel and Howard Barker, with whose work he is especially associated as a founder member of the Wrestling School. He has composed theatre songs with, among others, Andy Hamilton, Nick Dark and Tony Harrison, and his music is performed frequently in Europe and the US. Parallel with his theatre work, Matthew works widely in television and film. Further information is posted on his website: www.matthewscott.net

Words: Mark Ravenhill

Opening Act One

Music: Matthew Scott

Opening Act One

C ♩ = 130

D TUTTI (in two parts)

En - ter - prise come light our dark - ness Bus' - ness shape our heart and hand

Then oh rich our Fath-er migh- ty Lead us to the Prom - ised land

♩ = 120

Words: Mark Ravenhill

Music: Matthew Scott

Funeral, Motto 2 and Wake

Funeral Motto 2 and Wake

gone   But   tears won't bring back milk that's spilt and the wid - ow carr - ies

B

on, the Wid - ow carr - ies   on

TAMBOURINE (onstage)

WHISTLE (onstage)

f   Cm   G

Cm   G   Cm   B♭   E♭   Fm   G   Cm   G

Cm   G   Cm   Cm   G   Cm   G   Cm   B♭

WHISTLE (onstage)

E♭   Fm   G   Cm   G   Cm   G   Cm

crumble on cue

Music: Matthew Scott

Wake 2

Music: Matthew Scott

Wake 3

Motto 3 and Eros' Song 1

Words: Mark Ravenhill

Music: Matthew Scott

120

Motto Three

day._____ His wa-gon burn-ing bright,_____ For once di-ur-nal course is run Comes E-ros and the night._____ A-rise you swain, no slum-ber ing_____ Oh heed the call of__ night._____

Motto Three

My ar - row's sharp, my bow is stretched, Here's E - ros here's de - light.

E   C/E   F#sus   Am/C   Bsus   C△

A - rise,____ a - rise,____ Up up and rise and

Bsus   Em   Am   F/A   Am

rise and ri - sen fol - low me.____ And ri - sen fol low__

F   Dm   Esus   E   F   C

122

ri - sen fol low_ and ri - sen fol - low me.

Motto Three

D (Scene changes

Clarinets

(+ Elec Gtr / Crotales)

Am   C/E   Dm/F   E⁷   Am

Let

Sus Cy

E - ros   guide   you   through   the   streets_____   To   ev - 'ry   man   a

Sax 1

F/A   Am   G/B   C

Motto Three

Motto Three

Motto Three

Motto 4: New Stock

Words: Mark Ravenhill

Music: Matthew Sc

Words: Mark Ravenhill

Music: Matthew Sco

Motto Five: Dame Fortune

End of Act One

Words: Mark Ravenhill

Music: Matthew Scott

Rejoice - End of Act One

131

Rejoice - End of Act One

134

Rejoice - End of Act One

END OF ACT ON

PHOEBUS Reprise

Words: Mark Ravenhill

Music: Matthew Scott

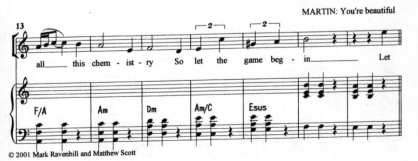

136

Phoebus Reprise

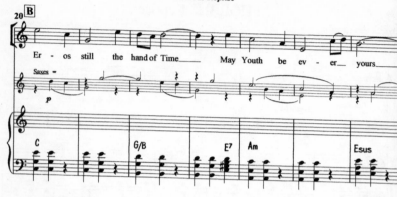

Er - os still the hand of Time___ May Youth be ev - er___ yours___

Saxes =

C   G/B   E7   Am   Esus

— With Age comes grief but youth is free so play___ and

E   C/E   F#sus   Am/C   Bsus   CΔ

Enter MOLLIES   (BLIND MANS BLUFF)

leave re - morse

[+Cym]

Bsus   Em

Phoebus Reprise

Words: Mark Ravenhill

Mother Claps Maggot

Music: Matthew Scott

(Jig pre-Fine Fucking)

Words: Mark Ravenhill

Music: Matthew Scott

Fine Fucking

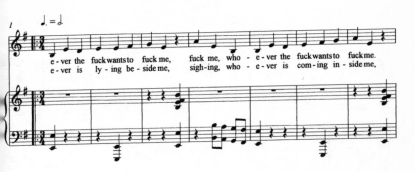

e - ver the fuck wants to fuck me, fuck me, who - e - ver the fuck wants to fuck me.
e - ver is ly - ing be - side me, sigh-ing, who - e - ver is com - ing in - side me,

Fuck me 'cos you are the fi - nest, the fi - nest I've fucked, the fi - nest, the
dy - ing, the stran - ger, the stran - ger I'm fuck-ing the bet - ter, but clo - sing my

allargando - - - - -

fi - nest, the fi - nest I've fucked. Who - still see your face, so we'll
eyes,____ I

Fine Fucking

Birthing Scene

Music: Matthew Scott

Segue "Pleasure"

142

Pleasure

Words: Mark Ravenhill

Music: Matthew Scott

144

145

Pleasure

REPEAT AND F

The Whore's Prayer

Words: Mark Ravenhill

Music: Matthew Scott

Bolton
Fa - ther look down on your chil - dren now all the cus - to - mers have gone.

Cranton
Fa - ther look down on our bro - thel emp - ty, how shall we car - ry on?
Ev - 'ry man's turned Mol - ly, and

148

The Whore's Prayer

ev-'ry maid's a-lone. Fa-ther bring them back from So-dom. Bring the bug-gers home, bring the

bug-gers home.

Fa-ther fill your bro-thels 'til they're brim-ming, show us joy once more.

The Whore's Prayer

Fa - ther don't a - ban - don me, or me, or me, or me, an ho - nest sim - ple whore.

Worl - d'll soon be emp - ty if ev - 'ry man's turned queer.

Man must sport with maid a - gain oh

Bring the bug - gers here, bring the bug - gers here.

Words: Mark Ravenhill

Music: Matthew Scott

Motto Six

GOD:
The pain of love is hard to bear

Clarinets

The joy of love is strong   And   lov - ers come and fuck and leave   but

bus' ness carr - ies on,   Oh bus' ness carr - ies   on

Motto Six 29-8-01

En - ter - prise shall light your dark - ness Bus' ness must go

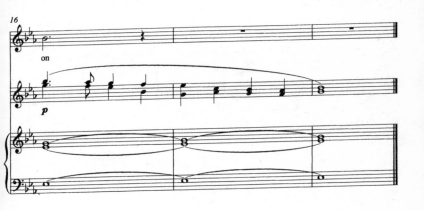

on

Music: Matthew Sco

Amelia's Maggot

Segue Club Music